The Potency of the Principalship: Action-Oriented Leadership at the Heart of School Improvement

Nicholas D. Young
Elizabeth Jean
Anne E. Mead

Series in Education

Copyright © 2019 Vernon Press, an imprint of Vernon Art and Science Inc, on behalf of the author.

All rights reserved. No part of this publication may be reproduced, stored in a retrieval system, or transmitted in any form or by any means, electronic, mechanical, photocopying, recording, or otherwise, without the prior permission of Vernon Art and Science Inc.

www.vernonpress.com

In the Americas:
Vernon Press
1000 N West Street,
Suite 1200, Wilmington,
Delaware 19801
United States

In the rest of the world:
Vernon Press
C/Sancti Espiritu 17,
Malaga, 29006
Spain

Series in Education

Library of Congress Control Number: 2018952658

ISBN: 978-1-62273-709-3

Also available:

Hardback: 978-1-62273-444-3

E-book: 978-1-62273-552-5

Product and company names mentioned in this work are the trademarks of their respective owners. While every care has been taken in preparing this work, neither the authors nor Vernon Art and Science Inc. may be held responsible for any loss or damage caused or alleged to be caused directly or indirectly by the information contained in it.

Every effort has been made to trace all copyright holders, but if any have been inadvertently overlooked the publisher will be pleased to include any necessary credits in any subsequent reprint or edition.

Acknowledgement

It is with sincere gratitude and deep appreciation that we begin this book by thanking Mrs. Suzanne "Sue" Clark for her editorial assistance that made this manuscript stronger. She has a gifted mind and swift hand and has been the primary editor of more of our books then we can remember. Let the public record reflect that we recognize her substantial contributions to this tome, and our volume of work, more than she may realize. Beyond acknowledging her unmatched professional skills, even more importantly, we consider her an exceptional friend.

Table of Contents

Acknowledgement		iii
Foreword		vii
Preface		xi
Chapter 1	**Promoting Passion in Others: Recruiting, Evaluating, and Retaining a High-Performance Team**	1
Chapter 2	**Learning the Lingo: Professional Development to Increase Student Growth**	17
Chapter 3	**Leveraging the Role of Teacher Unions: Striving for Collaboration and Mutual Respect**	25
Chapter 4	**Goal Setting to Raise the Bar: Improving the School from Within**	37
Chapter 5	**The Critical Nature of Data Driven Decision Making: Improving Academic Performance through Analytics**	45
Chapter 6	**Earning an 'A' in Instructional Leadership: Promoting Continuous Improvement Through Deliberate Practices**	59
Chapter 7	**Valuing Equity, Equality, and Inclusive Practices: Fostering Achievement in Diverse Populations**	71
Chapter 8	**Tapping Technology: Standards and Instructional Practices with Promise**	83
Chapter 9	**Your House or Mine: Meeting Families at the Front Door**	95

| Chapter 10 | **The Importance of School Law: Positive Outcomes for All Students** | 115 |
| Chapter 11 | **Resources at your Fingertips** | 127 |

References 131

About the Authors 153

Foreword

As part of her third grade Social Studies curriculum, my daughter recently went on a field trip designed to explore historical landmarks within our Connecticut town. One of their first stops was a tour of the Wallop School Museum, a one room, brick schoolhouse built in 1800 and currently maintained by the Enfield Historical Society. While she excitedly shared the details of handmade wooden and metal desks built to seat two students and the fact that students were required to carry in the firewood used to heat their schoolhouse, my mind explored how these early learning environments had morphed into our modern day public schools.

Given the professional conversations and interactions that I had with the school leaders in my district earlier that day, I was especially focused on the responsibilities of current principals. Conversations regarding the integration of virtual reality software, teacher evaluation, school safety drills, benchmark assessments, and the use of social media platforms to communicate with parents and community members had clearly delineated the stark differences between the responsibilities of today's school leaders and those associated with the earliest schools. Further consideration on the topic highlighted the fact that the one room schoolhouse was the starting point of an educational timeline that has witnessed a complete transformation of the role of the school principal, with significant changes happening almost annually as a result of myriad economic, political, societal, and community events and circumstances.

According to the Wallace Foundation (2013), the five key functions of principal leadership are establishing a vision of academic success for all students, creating a climate that supports learning, developing leadership within the school, improving instructional practice and managing resources in order to reach the established vision. Multiple research findings have confirmed that school leadership is the second most important school-based factor in a child's academic achievement, second only to teacher effectiveness (Wallace Foundation, 2013; National Association of Secondary School Principals and National Association of Elementary School Principals, 2013).

Anyone who has recently spent time in a school, especially those schools struggling with the effects of poverty, knows that the key functions of a school principal are much easier to write about than to actually achieve. The work of a 21st century school principal requires an individual to simultaneously be a visionary and a conformist, a leader and a follower, an inspiration and a task master. The contradictory nature of the role comes from principals having a range of leadership responsibilities while filling the middle management rung on their district's organizational ladder. They are held accountable for leading their buildings forward to new levels of practice and student achievement while simultaneously asked to ensure that the district's vision, however traditional, is clearly evident in their approach. They may be asked to adhere to the policies and procedures adopted by their school district in response to a past event or legislative movement, while simultaneously tasked to be forward thinking in their improvement efforts.

Developing and sustaining a school vision that mandates academic success for all students is both noble and moral; yet this effort is further complicated by federal and state mandates seeking to eliminate achievement gaps that exist across the country for students identified in racial and socioeconomic subgroups. Hansen, Levesque, Quintero, and Valant (2018) looked at the latest National Assessment of Education Progress (NAEP) results, to discover that the nation has made progress over the past decade narrowing the achievement gap between white students and their black and Hispanic counterparts yet has failed to close the gap between students living in poverty and their wealthier cohort. While the teachers and staff members in a given building are obviously sharing in the efforts to ensure equity in achievement, the contributions of a school principal are often highly scrutinized despite national trends suggesting the difficulty of such an undertaking. The educational leaders of our earliest schools could not have imagined the level of accountability related to student achievement that would become commonplace for our modern-day principals.

Principals are charged with developing and supporting a vision of academic success for all as well as with ensuring the school climate is conducive to learning. This climate is the foundation by which all school improvements are built. Principals who develop climates that value and empower teachers and students will be more likely to maximize their instructional time and regularly produce tangible examples of student learning. To do this effectively, school principals must address classroom management, inclusive practices, staff collaboration, student discipline, parent communication, data analysis and scheduling to name just a few. As one would imagine, any of the aforementioned topics could by itself require a great deal of time, human capital and fiscal resources (National Association of Secondary School Principals and National Association of Elementary School Principals, 2013).

Most principals, however, are expected to address several of these key areas concurrently, while also acting as the primary disciplinarian and parent contact of their school. In larger schools where a team of principals and vice principals share these duties, the principal is then responsible for monitoring the effectiveness of the team and its individual as well.

Principals must work collaboratively with students, teachers, support personnel, families and the community at large in order to ensure a school climate and culture that supports their academic vision. Modern day societal circumstances are often working against the school principals as a recent survey reports that more than half of the nation's children below the age of 12 have experienced one or more forms of serious trauma (U.S. Department of Health and Human Services, Health Resources and Services Administration, Maternal and Child Health Bureau, 2014). This statistic has significant implications on the kinds of learning environments our students require, the types of behaviors they exhibit and the likelihood they will achieve grade level expectations. Nonetheless, principals are charged to develop and maintain a school culture that affirms the worth and diversity of all its members, thereby ensuring they reach their fullest potential.

On a national scale, the recent teacher evaluation movement has more clearly defined the systematic process of teacher accountability used to reach the achievement goals that guide the work of our principals (Huber & Skedsmo, 2016). The level with which a school leader provides instructional leadership is a key factor in school and district success. Instructional leadership is a series of actions that positively contribute to the consistent implementation of research-based practices within a school. The school principal is often the only staff member to actually observe the entire teaching staff; thus, the modern-day principal is expected to have expertise in curriculum, instruction, assessment, and classroom environments. By developing the kinds of relationships that allow teachers to be open to receiving actionable feedback, building principals can ensure high quality instruction is delivered on a daily basis in their classrooms.

Principals are also expected to provide meaningful professional development, encourage staff members to observe expert colleagues in action, and support coaching and mentoring opportunities with and amongst their staff members (National Association of Secondary School Principals and National Association of Elementary School Principals, 2013). It is through the lens of instructional leadership that principals are able to be the kind of inspirational cheerleader that motivates teachers to take risks that will improve their instructional practice. Opportunities to delegate and share leadership responsibilities centered on instructional improvements are also a prudent decision given the level of accountability and the limited time school principals have.

Principals who work to develop teacher leaders and functional teacher teams within their buildings will increase the likelihood that the change effort is organically grown and maintained. While instructional leadership and the development of a shared leadership model requires a steep time commitment, principals who positively increase the collective efficacy of their staff members are more likely to see higher results in student achievement and staff satisfaction. Unfortunately, things like school safety concerns and student discipline often pull principals away from the very classrooms that need the instructional leadership they are required to provide.

Today's school principals are asked to lead and follow simultaneously, leaving them metaphorically with one foot in the past and a foot in the future. This phenomenon is further complicated by the necessary juggling of both time and energy on a lengthy list of daily responsibilities within their schools. While this realistic description may make the role seem daunting, the reality is that the impact of an effective school principal is almost palpable when you walk through the doors of a school. While vastly different than the simple role of our earliest school leaders, the personality of today's principal becomes inextricably woven throughout the culture of the building as they are directly and indirectly connected to all of the decisions made within that school.

The Potency of the Principalship: Action-Oriented Leadership at the Heart of School Improvement recognizes the profound impact that an effective principal can have on a community of learners in the 21st century and the challenges that accompany this critical role. Unlike many other books written about one particular aspect of school leadership, this reference guide provides a variety of practical tools and tasks directly linked to the responsibilities of the school principal. Understanding the need for principals to continually produce higher levels of student achievement, it walks its readers through a series of key areas that will directly and indirectly impact student performance while acknowledging the ever-changing demographic profiles of our students and families, the increased emphasis on instructional leadership and the need for technology integration and effective community outreach. *The Potency of the Principalship: Action-Oriented Leadership at the Heart of School Improvement* strategically places the principal in the center of an interconnected web of key leadership focus areas and is designed to prevent school principals, and those supporting their efforts, from becoming obsolete like the one room schoolhouse or the handmade desks for two.

Tracy A. Youngberg, Ed.D.
Connecticut National Distinguished Principal of the Year
Assistant Superintendent of Teaching, Learning, and Leadership,
Windham Public Schools

Preface

The Potency of the Principalship: Action-Oriented Leadership at the Heart of School Improvement is a book written for building and district administrators, aspiring school leaders, graduate education students, educational policymakers, education professors, and school practitioners who are interested in the evolving principal role and/or the potential of this position to facilitate substantial student and school achievement. It reflects a keen understanding of the most important ideas in administrative leadership to date and guides the reader on a comprehensive journey through the diverse responsibilities of the 21st century principal.

While there are numerous books describing leadership tasks and styles, this tome delves into the very heart of leadership and how the alignment of myriad responsibilities positively influences student outcomes. As such, our motivation for writing this book comes from the following:

- *Our desire to inform the reader that the role of principal has changed dramatically and, concurrently, principal expectations have multiplied, while the time for any given task has been minimized;*
- *Our interest in sharing principal best practices that will influence teacher praxis; thus, having an immediate impact on student attainment of skills and knowledge;*
- *Our knowledge that principals help to create excellent teachers when professional development opportunities are sustained throughout the year, when adequate time is allocated to practice skills learned, and when actionable feedback is provided;*
- *Our awareness, through experience and a careful examination of relevant research, that a successful principal must actively engage families and community-based members to ensure student success;*
- *Our belief that, despite the many administrative duties and necessary requirements that come along with the principalship, school leaders must be passionate about their work;*
- *Our understanding that when principals guide and support all educators, they can achieve building-wide student academic proficiency; and*
- *Our deep commitment to shaping a vision of education that is inclusive, personalized, and focuses on the needs of all students.*

Most principals are tasked with leading a large group of individuals with varied beliefs, educational backgrounds, expertise, and expectations; yet it is worth acknowledging that teachers and paraprofessionals are assumed to have entered the field with a belief that they can make a positive difference and have a strong desire to educate the next generation (Young, Bonanno-Sotiropoulos, & Smolinski, 2018b). In this cauldron of ideas and expectations, success must begin with a sense of purpose (Sinek, 2011). This clarity of purpose is the building block for a string of others that, in turn, encompass who a principal is and what a principal does.

A principal is responsible for budgets, discipline, assessment, observation and evaluation, engaging with families and the community, as well as a host of other items; yet those are merely the tasks that fall under the job title. To inspire others, a principal must connect the work to why they do what they do – that is their sense of purpose (Blanchard & Broadwell, 2018; Sinek, Mead, & Docker, 2017). Once the purpose is clearly defined, they can move to the strategy or approach that will be used to engage all staff; while, finally, principals will add the tools that attract the employees to think and work in a particular way (Sinek et al., 2017; Rasmussen, 2016).

It is easy to say that that administrators and teachers believe they can make a difference; however, it is only through the creation of a bold purpose statement that the belief becomes a reality (Sinek, 2011). Therefore, to use the example by Rasmussen (2016), an enlightened principal might say

> *Everything we do, we believe in challenging our students' thinking. We believe in inquiry. The way we challenge our students is by making our school safe and innovative, with passionate and knowledgeable teachers who are caring and compassionate, who cater to the needs of all students. And, we happen to graduate honorable and educated citizens (n.p.).*

This sounds vastly different from the principal who comes to work each day merely for the paycheck, who has settled for the status quo, and does not engage staff in a common purpose. That principal might say "We teach high school. Our culture is spirited and sound. Our curriculum is rich. Our test scores are high" (Rasmussen, 2016, n.p.). Who would you follow?

School leaders who are passionate about making a difference to the lives of others, bring a high level of energy to the task (Burgess & Houf, 2017). These same principals lead with love and have a well-articulated and clear purpose that inspires their faculty to teach at a higher level and their students to believe in themselves and their power to learn despite obstacles (Grundler & Grundler, 2017). There is an undeniable belief in building a positive school culture that will transform all who are willing to put in equal effort, and this is palpable to staff, students, family and community members.

Those who aspire to lead in this way are usually referred to as servant or transformational leaders, while those in the position for the power or glory are often referred to as autocratic leaders. Servant or transformational leaders put the needs and well-being of others first and help to develop their skills; thus, the culture provides security, a sense of autonomy, and the freedom and safety to ask for assistance when needed (Greenleaf Center for Servant Leadership, 2016).

Principals who serve their staff lead by example to "raise one another to higher levels of morality and motivation" (Burns, 1978). They believe that it is their job to model and encourage academic, social, and behavioral greatness. Those who "serve-first" instead of "lead first" (Greenleaf Center for Servant Leadership, 2016, n.p.) set clear goals and have high expectations for their staff; yet support, encouragement, and recognition are provided to ensure everyone achieves these lofty ideals (Bass & Riggio, 2014; Hoerr, 2005). Leaders, therefore, especially for principals who want to see high levels of sustained change, must think, act, and communicate differently (Sinek et al., 2017).

Entwined with being a transformational leader, these same principals are tasked with being instructional leaders. Here the focus is on management of assets such as using resources effectively and being an instructional resource as well as servant-first characteristics such as being a role model for staff, having communication skills that "inspire trust, spark motivation and empower teachers and students" (Concordia University-Portland, 2018, n.p.). This is a tall order. Principals spend a great deal of time being both a servant and an instructional leader, while simultaneously being a master negotiator, a diplomat, and more – often within the span of a single day (Concordia University-Portland, 2018). Finding balance can be difficult, if not impossible, thus, another necessary skill for any well-rounded principal is time management.

It has been argued that in order to affect whole-school improvement it is more important to develop high-quality leaders rather than individual teachers due to the over-arching influence that belongs to the principal (Jensen, Downing, & Clark, 2017). For this reason, principals must be experts at communication, ensuring professional development that is sustained and driven towards improving teacher practices as well as academic achievement, inspiring others to become leaders themselves, bringing together families and community members to increase school opportunities, and partnering with unions to support staff and student success (Jensen et al., 2017).

The authors are deeply concerned about the principalship as they are invested members of educational teams themselves: at one time or another having been a teacher, director, administrator, principal, and/or a superintendent as well as college professor and dean of education. With a rich and long history of leadership between them, the authors hope to reinvigorate current administrators and inspire the next generation of educational leaders to become inspirational, impactful, and engaging in their own right.

It is not surprising, then, that this book takes a critical and comprehensive look at the myriad issues mentioned and offers equal parts history and strategy as a means to encourage and sustain principals and others interested in the field. The role of the school leader is vital to the success of staff and students alike; therefore, it behooves all of us to better understand, assist, and support those who assume this position of great responsibility.

Chapter 1

Promoting Passion in Others: Recruiting, Evaluating, and Retaining a High-Performance Team

Staffing a school is a complicated process. There are challenges with finding committed teachers with the proper credentials within established budget constricts as well as retaining these highly qualified faculty - especially for those with specialized training in the Science, Technology, Engineering and Mathematics (STEM) fields who can be easily pulled away by promising careers in industry (Ronfeldt, 2012). The needs of teachers at different phases of the career cycle complicate professional development and merely considering the needs of teachers starting out, in isolation, provides some hint at the complexity of staffing schoolwide.

Early career educators encounter unique problems. Whether or not they progress to full time teachers depends on various factors, such as the conditions specific to the school setting and support they receive during training sessions and the school year in general (Feiman-Nemser, 2012; Ronfeldt, 2012). Regardless of the level of experience in the profession, the good news is that teacher retention can be improved through supportive leadership, appropriate compensation, and the use of teacher evaluations that give comprehensive, personalized feedback to improve teaching practices (You, Kim, & Lim, 2017; Darling-Hammond, Beardsley, Haertel, & Rothstein, 2011). As if this were not enough to keep in mind, effective schools run by engaged leaders promote continuous improvement, including lifelong professional development processes for teachers from preservice thru retirement.

Impact of Hiring

Staffing within a school can greatly affect whether or not that school succeeds, and research shows that effective schools tend to follow certain hiring trends (Loeb, Kalogrides, & Beteille, 2012). These schools are inclined to attract effective teachers from other schools; and when new teachers are hired, they are ideally assigned to classes in such a way so as to not overburden them. Effective schools hire teachers who are capable of raising achievement performance in a relatively brief period, suggesting the positive impact that good teachers might have (Loeb et al., 2012). Further, Loeb et al. (2012) proved that stronger schools were able to retain their high-quality hires rather than lose them to turnover. These findings suggest how effective schools differentiated themselves from ineffective schools and demonstrated the value of employing and retaining effective teachers (Loeb et al., 2012). For these reasons, principals must make difficult decisions regarding staffing and school organization that then effects other aspects of the building and culture.

By following best practices and attempting to meet the needs of teachers, principals can help to lure talented instructors and retain them for the long term. These needs range from providing effective administrative support to providing sufficient salaries (Partee, 2014; You et al., 2017; Hendricks, 2014). Evaluation is also considered important to both principals and teachers who feel it assists their ability to improve their own instructional delivery; yet it is impossible to evaluate staff until quality faculty members have been retained (Taylor & Tyler, 2012).

Early Career Teachers

Teachers entering the field encounter problems that, while similar to those with more experience, are magnified by a lack of specific supportive resources for first year or new faculty (Feiman-Nemser, 2012). Newly hired staff may find themselves mired by a range of problems that can dissuade them from staying on at a school to include struggles in creating relationships with students, difficulties managing school bureaucracy, and a lack of understanding of how to apply pedagogical techniques (Feiman-Nemser, 2012).

The problems for novices are compounded at larger schools, as well as vocational schools, where they are more likely to have poor perceptions of their own self-efficacy (Meristo & Eisenschmidt, 2014). Novice teachers at smaller schools may avoid this pitfall if they are provided adequate formal and informal collegial mentorship to help them learn the ropes; however, their self-efficacy perceptions can also be improved with a supportive work climate fostered by the building leadership (Meristo & Eisenschmidt, 2014).

New teachers have been compared to individuals marooned on a desert island, often facing a plethora of challenges without a clear direction or helping hand; thus, support becomes imperative (Feiman-Nemser, 2012). Difficulties can dissuade people from continuing within the teaching profession, and although retention continues to be important from one year to another, the early years, in particular, are an intense time in which the novice is continuing to learn and apply what he or she was taught during his or her preservice experience (Feiman-Nemser, 2012). It can also be a lonely period, which makes it a risky one for retention; thus, principals seeking to foster high performing teams need to be particularly vigilant about providing assistance and supportive structures for novice teachers during those early years.

Preservice Teachers

Prior to formally entering the teaching field, preservice teachers practice and observe instructional methods while acting as student teachers (Ronfeldt, 2012). These preservice professionals, still participating in their education programs, visit schools and observe tenured teachers as they go about their work. Student teachers also interact with students and acquire invaluable experience in many areas. Once employed as teachers, however, they may or may not be successfully retained (Ronfeldt, 2012). Retention can be positively impacted if student teachers spend their practice period working at schools that have more tenured teachers, presumably because a more veteran staff if better equipped to share the essential tips and strategies needed to be successful and or to feel better connected to the craft. While principals from harder to staff schools might welcome the opportunity to have student teachers in the classroom, practicing in such schools negatively influences retention of these individuals once in their own classroom.

With regard to the working environment, the well-being of student teachers can be promoted through emotional and informational support that leads to personal empowerment (Vaisanen, Pietarinen, Pyhalto, Toom, & Soini, 2016). Qualitative exploration of the experiences of student teachers revealed that their experiences were a blend of empowerment and insecurity (Vaisanen et al., 2016). Their well-being was promoted when there was sufficient informational support from both peers and superiors that provided the necessary basis for student teachers to engage in tasks centered on the academic and social concerns of their students and the school. The lack of social support they described was a point of concern, as it would directly lead to an improved sense of well-being. The importance of supportive environments was reinforced by the examination of easy to staff schools as preservice teachers who practiced in such environments were more likely to be retained (Ronfeldt, 2012).

Retaining Novice and Early Career Teachers

Numerous factors influence the retention of novice and early career teachers to include professional behaviors, collegiality, professional development, physical and emotional isolation, workload, classroom behaviors, and a support system that includes mentorship (Buonomo, Fatigante, & Fiorilli, 2017). A study of teachers in Korea validated this finding, with results demonstrating that teachers felt a greater sense of job satisfaction when they received adequate support from both their colleagues and leaders (You et al., 2017). Such a finding would suggest that principals play a significant role in improving teacher satisfaction as they can provide the support necessary to increase the satisfaction that teachers feel in their jobs.

Physical and Emotional Isolation

Teacher isolation was a major contributing factor in retention difficulties according to Buchanan et al. (2013). According to the research, teachers felt physically isolated in the classroom without the support of other faculty members who could lend a supportive ear when they were discouraged or unsure (Buchanan et al., 2013). In schools where there were few opportunities to communicate across the organization, the problems were particularly heightened (Buchanan et al., 2013).

While physical isolation created a discouraging condition, teachers sometimes felt professionally and emotionally isolated as well (Ostovar-Nameghi & Sheikhahmadi, 2016). Teachers who were the only instructors of a subject often felt professionally isolated. Emotionally, new teachers were prone to feeling isolated as they were afraid to fail, while more seasoned teachers were more likely to cope with emotional loneliness more effectively (Buchanan et al., 2013).

Professional Development

With regard to professional issues in school, new teachers wanted a chance to experience professional development and expected there to be opportunities to grow within their field (Buchanan et al., 2013). Consistent with the desire to feel professionally connected within their organization; they expressed a desire to collaborate with and learn from their peers (Mirel & Goldin, 2012). Consequently, failing to deliver opportunities to teachers that enable them to grow may lead to educator flight. Also notable is that while teachers do want the chance to connect with other professionals within their organizations, they also desire a chance to connect with teachers from other schools (Buchanan et al., 2013).

Classroom Behaviors

Within the classroom, behavior management may impact whether a teacher decides to stay at a school. Teachers reported feeling they were not prepared properly to manage the behaviors of students. Training programs revolved around other areas, like instructional delivery, rather than on managing unruly behavior. New teachers sometimes may feel targeted by the student population, which can dissuade them from remaining at a school (Riggio, 2017).

Another negative impact on the decision to stay was the perception that school policies prevent the discipline of badly behaved students, such as preventing expulsion for even the most negative behavior (Riggio, 2017).

Workload Expectations

New teachers sometimes felt overwhelmed by the amount of work they were expected to complete in their first year as a teacher leading to an overall negative experience (Hazell, 2017). Those in the study felt challenged by having to prepare the materials they needed to for their classes as well as being asked to fulfill duties that were outside of their areas of expertise (Buchanan et al., 2013). For instance, teachers were asked to take on administrative duties not typically expected of them, in addition to their teaching workload, while at other times, teachers taught subjects they were not familiar with (Hazell, 2017). A high workload was negatively associated with retention among new teachers; however, a high workload was also associated with lower retention levels among teachers in general (Hughes, 2012; Buchanan et al., 2013). Excessive workloads tend to drive teachers out of the school system, either in attempts to find employment in other organizations or as part of retirement from the field entirely (Hughes, 2012).

Educator Resiliency

The degree of resilience a teacher has toward negative circumstances within their profession may predict whether they are retained, and this effect is particularly pronounced among novice teachers (Doney, 2013). As such, principals will benefit from fostering the development of further resilience among their staff (Benjamin & Black, 2012). Resilience develops as the result of high pressure and stress and the ability to cope with them within the workplace (Benjamin & Black, 2012). Teachers draw upon protective factors to support them against the negative impact of stressors. The results of the Doney (2013) study suggest that principals should maximize the number of protective factors available within the school environment.

It is particularly important that principals structure the first year of a novice teacher such that shared obstacles and difficulties are encountered within the context of the common protective factors necessary for overcoming these stressors (Buonomo et al., 2017). In doing so, principals can create the conditions that make it far more likely a novice teacher will stay beyond the first year. The resilience that a teacher develops in that first year will be a resource drawn upon in subsequent years, encouraging the likelihood of retention for the long term (Doney, 2013).

Administrative Leadership

Principals are tasked with creating the kind of work environment that is conducive to creating a supportive environment (You et al., 2017). Consequently, both in their personal actions and in the environment they create, principals provide the supportive context that creates feelings of job satisfaction. By engaging with teachers and showing that they support them, principals can help to address issues not related to salary (Curtis, 2012). The need for administrative support has been shown in other studies (Partee, 2014; You et al., 2017). The findings by Curtis (2012) reinforced the important role that administrators can play in helping retain specific content area teachers.

Administrative support is important in retaining teachers (Lynch, 2012). In some cases, teachers report feeling bullied by their superiors or feeling undervalued. Regardless of these feelings, teachers in these circumstances are more inclined to leave their jobs. Principals should be aware of various factors that make it likely for teachers to depart and take action to address that, particularly in areas of increased administrative support and decision-making (Partee, 2014).

This again suggested how important a positive, supportive administration is to retaining staff (Lynch, 2012). Administrators may cause hostile environments that push teachers away through behaviors that are disengaged or otherwise not supportive. They may also fail to provide adequate observations that help teachers improve. Under these circumstances, teachers are inclined to leave their jobs rather than attempt to stay. Acting in a supportive manner can be one of the most direct ways that administrators can effect change within their organizations and encourage retention (Lynch, 2012).

Salary

Another fact that can negatively affect the likeliness of retaining a teacher is low salary (Hughes, 2012). Feeling underpaid can lead to dissatisfaction and the decision to leave a school for other employment. Research suggests that increasing a teacher's pay reduces the chance of teacher turnover, and this effect is pronounced among newer teachers (Hendricks, 2014). The simple act of increasing pay reduces attrition, which has the secondary effect of increasing student academic achievement. Salary is often negotiated by the union; however, leaving the superintendent and principal with little control in this area.

The experience a teacher brought to the classroom was associated with increased student performance, and so simply paying teachers more might be an effective means of improving schoolwide performance (Hendricks, 2014). This improvement attached to increased salary was observed up to 19 years into a teacher's career, suggesting it was an effective means of reducing attrition and improving achievement for nearly two decades (Hendricks, 2014). Conversely, paying teachers less is more likely to encourage attrition. A combination of high workload and low pay creates the perfect circumstances in which to drive teachers out of a school (Hendricks, 2014).

Salary incentivizes retention (Lynch, 2012). Missouri schools used an advancement framework known as the Career Ladder; under this framework, teachers could improve from observations and take on additional responsibilities (Lynch, 2012). By meeting both state and district performance standards, they became eligible for increased responsibilities or professional development programs that were accompanied by pay increases.

Using the Career Ladder method, teachers were given incentives to improve. When teachers performed their duties adequately according to observers, they were given pay increases (Lynch, 2012). This placed the salary increases of a teacher partly under the control of the teacher. This program engaged teachers, afforded chances to increase salary, and provided opportunities for professional development (Lynch, 2012). These opportunities were associated with increased retention as well, suggested that such incentive programs that afforded professional development might be a mean of promoting retention.

Specific Teacher Populations

There may also be segments of the teaching population that are specifically disposed to higher attrition than others (Ingersoll, Merrill, & May 2012). A study of teachers revealed that pedagogical training was an important predictor in retention; however, a teacher who entered either math or science education fields received, on average, less pedagogical training (Ingersoll et al., 2012). Consequently, the likeliness of math or science teachers leaving a school was higher than among teachers in other fields (Ingersoll et al., 2012). After the first year of education, the attrition rates for these teachers remained higher than among their peers necessitating principals to pay specific attention to this demographic. Principals may need to provide additional training specific to these faculty members in order to reduce the chance of their leaving a school for other work.

Curtis (2012) noted that math teachers originally entered the profession because they enjoyed working with young people. Specifically, they hoped to pass on their own love of learning and make a difference in the students' lives; however, they often end up leaving due to a combination of factors that include low salary, poor administrative support, and the tendency to place the blame of a lack of academic success heavily on a teacher's shoulders (Curtis, 2012).

Administrators can provide a significant amount of support and resources that may help ensure retention (Curtis, 2012).

Teachers of color are another educator demographic targeted to promote increased retention (Partee, 2014). This requires promoting higher retention rates in schools in general; however, it is also important to note that there may be specific challenges for this group. Teachers of color may feel inadequate preparation should they enter the teaching field through alternate routes (Carver-Thomas, 2018). These same teachers may work in high poverty, urban communities where they are more likely to earn lower salaries than teachers operating in low poverty districts. In order to retain teachers of color, preservice scholarships and loan forgiveness, teacher residencies, partnering with local colleges, 'grow-your-own' district level programs, and comprehensive induction programs will all support the specific needs of this educator demographic (Carver-Thomas, 2018).

Challenging Schools

Another factor that influenced a teacher's desire to remain in a particular position included larger class sizes, concerns about school safety, fewer resources with which to work, higher rates of discipline issues, and lower levels of student achievement (Partee, 2014). Often, these teachers received lower levels of administrative support, had less autonomy in the classroom, and less influence on decision-making. This cluster of factors negatively affected teachers working in this environment and made it more likely they would leave. Challenging schools, in particular, may be locations where providing a mentor may benefit retention as these relationships afford early career teachers time to engage with others more experienced in the profession (Buchanan et al., 2013).

Despite the increased problems of operating in difficult schools, it is important to note that teachers persist at these organizations because they care (Petty, Fitchett, & O'Connor, 2012). It is true that salary is important and has been associated with increased retention; however, at least one study indicated most teachers remained out of loyalty to their students and their profession (Hendricks, 2014). The research findings did indicate that pay remained important to attracting teachers to high need schools; yet was less important than their loyalty (Petty et al., 2012). Principals should not underestimate the nontangible factors that draw teachers to these schools and cause them to remain, nor should they try to take advantage of those factors. Teachers care enough to remain at these schools with the highest demands. Salary plays the smaller part of how principals can support those teachers in order to retain them for the long term.

Separate research suggested that teachers leave difficult schools that have a larger concentration of minority and low-income students (Johnson, Kraft, & Papay, 2011). In these schools, working conditions tend to be more difficult (Partee, 2014). Teachers working in these environments generally report less job satisfaction and are more likely to have higher turnover intentions (Johnson et al., 2011). These schools may also suffer from organizational level characteristics that influence the retention of teachers. Such environments can broadly be characterized as unsupportive.

Despite beliefs that those at difficult schools are more likely to retire early, teachers in the lowest socioeconomic status schools were found to continue teaching until retirement at the same rate as those from the highest socioeconomic status schools (Hughes, 2012). These findings suggest that teacher intention to leave a position due to hardships in the school environment often does not translate tangible action, perhaps because it is increasingly difficult for senior teachers with higher salaries to find comparable positions elsewhere.

Retaining Veteran Teachers

Teacher retention has been discussed in at least one instance as an identity making process that requires career-long support (Schaefer, Long, & Clandinin, 2012). Professional identity for teachers is created at the beginning of a career; however, that identity may not be sustained throughout every year. Researchers suggested that personal and professional identities are constantly being negotiated (Schaefer et al., 2012). Early periods in a teaching career are often discussed in the existing research as learning a new role rather than taking on a new professional identity. Part of the means by which professional teaching identities are forged is through a mentoring relationship, which influences preservice teachers and increases confidence when the relationship is positive (Izadinia, 2015).

Even after such identities are forged, teachers continue to negotiate between their personal and professional identities until they are no longer able to identify with the teaching identity in the current education landscape (Schaefer et al., 2012). Little research has been conducted into studying identity formation among teachers but reducing teacher attrition may be accomplished by encouraging ongoing identification with the teaching identity. From this perspective, retention can be encouraged by considering the process one that involves sustaining teachers from their first year through to their last (Schaefer et al., 2012).

Creating continuous opportunities for teachers to identify closely with their professional roles may help to reduce attrition even at later stages of a career. Teachers also enjoy feeling that both students and parents are engaged as participant and cooperating with the education process (Hughes, 2012). Teachers want students to be interested in their own education. These teachers also want parents to be involved with the education of their children.

Evaluation

Evaluation is a part of the educator improvement and retention process designed to increase school outcomes. Specific state standards and means of evaluation vary from one state to another. The Massachusetts Department of Elementary and Secondary Education (2012), for example, details the standards it expects teachers to meet along a continuum where they are rated unsatisfactory, needs improvement, proficient, or exemplary. This rubric applies to four categories to include lesson planning and curriculum design, student outcomes, family engagement, and professional culture (Massachusetts Department of Elementary and Secondary Education, 2012).

Importantly, these standards are not meant to evaluate teachers solely according to academic outcomes, but also on classroom conditions and the learning environment a teacher promotes (Massachusetts Department of Elementary and Secondary Education, 2012). In a study by Jiang, Sporte, & Luppescu (2015), teachers appreciated actionable feedback and indicated that they believed there was a connection between the feedback they received from principals and their ability to deliver improved instruction (Jiang et al., 2015). At least one study indicated they responded positively for overhauls to the valuation methods applied to them, particularly with regard to increased observation of their performance in the classroom (Jiang et al., 2015). As such, evaluation has the potential to positively affect teacher performance.

Feedback

The use of actionable feedback ensured that there was improvement to classroom management, overall planning, use of assessments, differentiated instruction, and student focused learning (Massachusetts Department of Elementary and Secondary Education, 2012). Teacher evaluation systems were associated with positive outcomes such as instructional improvements, though there were specific best practices that were most likely to improve instructional ability, for instance, providing timely and focused feedback was considered important to improving instruction (Jiang et al., 2015)

Personalized. Observations of teachers should always include personalized feedback that is tailored to the individual's improvement (Taylor & Tyler, 2012). Such evaluation systems have the potential to help improve a teacher's instructional ability. A well-designed evaluation should be created to help inform teachers on improvement strategies and where to find the help they may need (Taylor & Tyler, 2012).

Interventions designed to introduce effective evaluations to a school can have varying effects, as demonstrated in one Chicago-based study (Steinberg & Sartain, 2015). The Excellence in Teaching Project started from a pilot program that included 44 elementary schools and expanded to 92 schools (Steinberg & Sartain, 2015). Prior to the program, teachers were evaluated using a checklist of classroom practices, with evaluators expecting teachers to hit every mark on the checklist to be successful. High performing teachers felt the checklist approach produced nothing in the way of individualized, meaningful feedback. The new evaluation program included classroom observation, discussions with teachers about teaching methods, and post-observation conferences (Steinberg & Sartain, 2015).

Principals held conferences with teachers, shared observations from the classroom, as well as discussed detailed feedback. This was consistent with the recommendations by Taylor and Tyler (2012), who noted that well designed evaluations should give personalized feedback. Academic outcomes were superior in more advantaged schools, indicating that other factors may be at play in less advantaged schools with regard to performance outcomes (Steinberg & Sartain, 2015). Other recommendations for creating an effective evaluation system include creating a system that integrates multiple classroom observations over the course of a year (Darling-Hammond et al., 2011). These programs give evaluators the chance to integrate multiple data points into their feedback and produce a better overall picture of a teacher's instructional practice.

Timeliness. Darling-Hammond et al. (2011) noted the importance for feedback to be timely. It should be given to teachers within a short time frame to ensure that improvements to instructional delivery could be maximized. An example of such a program would include up to six evaluations a year by mentors or principals. Following observations, evaluators meet relatively quickly with the teacher to discuss the findings. Others have also noted that there is a difference between simply rating performance and helping a teacher to develop (Marzano, 2012).

Assessment methods. Different assessment methods have different elements upon which a teacher can be identified (Marzano, 2012). A more rapid assessment designed to provide quick feedback on core skills must have a focused and limited set of evaluation categories; however, a more thorough assessment using broader criteria may help to assess a wide range of strengths and weaknesses (Marzano, 2012). Development of teachers should be the priority when implementing evaluations and a broader range of criteria may prove to help address and improve a teacher's instructional ability. This type of approach is consistent with high performance as schools that use evaluation for development, as opposed to accountability, saw vast improvements in school performance (Reinhorn, Johnson, & Simon, 2017).

Transformational Leadership

Principals who care deeply for their school's culture differentiate themselves as leaders versus others who are considered managers and administrators (Hollingworth, Olsen, Asikin-Garmager, Wimm, 2017). These same school leaders strive to foster positive school culture by building trusting relationships between and among their teaching staff (Gray, Kruse, & Tarter, 2016). These relationships, when based on shared values, assumptions, and beliefs and ideas that principals and teachers have about their schools, prove to be the foundation of a positive school culture (Hollingworth et al., 2017). Schools with a high level of trust, are those where collective decision-making is used, and interpersonal relationships between the principal and teachers create environments that are conducive to change (Louis & Murphy, 2017). The role of the principal, therefore, is moving beyond simply leading to a new style - that of transformational leadership.

The change in leadership style compels both principals and teachers to hold one another to higher levels of morality and motivation by inspiring one another to achieve higher organizational goals (Burns, 1978). Holistically, schools that use transformational leadership support those engaged in change and have found that they perform outside of originally contemplated targets (Veeriah, Piaw, Li, & Hoque, 2017). Leithwood (1992) stated that "transformational leadership facilitates the redefinition of a people's mission and vision, renewal of their commitment and the restructuring of their systems for goal accomplishment" (p. 11). Principals who lead to increase student learning understand and undertake changes in small increments, explain the reasons for proposed changes, help staff understand, and see high levels of cooperation by their staff; therefore, the school sees an increase in organizational change (Hollingworth et al., 2017).

Principal leadership that remains stable and builds trust over time is paramount to making changes within schools. Schools that experience high levels of leadership turnover lose faith in the system and, consequently, staff do not trust or implement changes easily. Teachers become apprehensive of too many leadership changes by showing feelings that mean, "here we go again" (Hollingworth et al., 2017, p. 8).

Supportive principals who allow teachers to take risks when trying new practices were acknowledged by teachers to be valued (Hollingworth et al.,

2017). Eliciting teacher buy-in prior to new changes assisted in getting other teachers to do the same, which in turn resulted in an easier transition, more fidelity in practice, and a shortened implementation timeline (Tschannen-Moran, 2016). These practices optimize transformational leadership and principals who wish to retain staff and increase student outcomes would be wise to follow such a path.

Beyond recognizing staff that can elicit buy in from others, principals who know their staff well have increased effectiveness with new initiatives (Veeria et al., 2017). Principals who are aware of each teacher's ability to lead instructional leadership initiatives and use them appropriately build cohesiveness with staff that leads to better outcomes for children through higher teaching morale and commitment (Grissom, Loeb, & Master, 2013).

It is only by building a "trusting and supportive relationship with teachers" (McLeskey & Waldron, 2015, p. 70) that the principal will be able to have teacher commitment and such commitment then drives the vision for a school (McLeskey & Waldron, 2015). School leaders who are focused and keep the vision clearly before them, will see a paradigm shift in their building practices towards more inclusive programs (Hollingworth et al., 2015).

Principals who put aside dedicated time and invest resources into building relationships realize sizeable pay-offs in the form of greater trust and respect between themselves and teachers. Having open discussions between teachers and principals where both sides can honor both the intent of criticism and the power of a disagreement as a source of growth will experience further trust-building (D'Auria, 2015). When teachers feel comfortable challenging the principal's decisions it should not be seen as negative; rather, it is a productive learning time that continues to build trust and validates that the principal is open to listening.

Time spent in the teaching trenches provides principals with valuable insights and ideas that can then be turned into actions that educators appreciate (Hollingworth et al., 2017). It is best to present theory-based innovative ideas to staff in a clear manner leaving time for questions and reflection (Hollingworth, et al., 2015). Once staff begin to accept new initiatives, principals should encourage individual teachers to try strategies based on research and proven practices. Though first attempts may fail, a strong, engaged principal will help teachers learn by mistakes made, and continued discussions will prove fruitful as errors turn into reliable action (D'Auria, 2015).

Engaging in purposeful bi-directional, daily communication will help to develop staff if they feel that there are clear expectations and up-to-date information regarding changes occurring in the school. This leads to further the sense of school cohesiveness and coherence towards learning goals (Mead,

2017). While many leadership styles are available to school leaders, those who espouse to be transformational, and follow the tenets, will find they have amassed a staff that is willing to follow and lead, collaborate and work autonomously, as well as work to the good of the organization as a whole, and more specifically, for students.

Final Thoughts

Preparing an adequate school staff requires preparation for teachers at the beginning of their careers, and throughout (Feiman-Nemser, 2012; Ronfeldt, 2012). Evaluations are a specific form of that ongoing development, and are best when personalized, comprehensive, and used primarily as a developmental tool (Marzano, 2012; Reinhorn et al., 2017; Taylor & Tyler, 2012). Beyond the development of teachers, successfully staffing a school and retaining that staff requires both a supportive environment and leadership (Buchanan et al., 2013; You et al., 2017). Using a transformational leadership style will enhance the likelihood of retaining teachers as the work environment is collaborative and uplifting. When a solid team is in place, and transformational leadership is the norm, schools will flourish, and students ultimately win.

Points to Remember

- *Effective schools hire teachers who can raise scores quickly and these same schools are more likely to retain high quality teachers.*
- *Early career teachers benefit from mentorship, professional development, and connections to staff. Retention depends on these factors in addition to a professional work environment.*
- *Teacher retention is a career-long, identity-making process that requires support from various stakeholders. In particular, mentoring preservice teachers increases feelings of positivity and confidence in abilities.*
- *Observations are an important part of the retention and improvement cycle. The principal and teacher should meet soon after the observation and discuss both what went well and what the weaknesses were. Evaluation systems that incorporate observations where the feedback is actionable and personalized help educators become more confident classroom facilitators.*
- *Principals who act from a transformational leadership role will find that the staff is more collaborative and works to ensure everyone's success. There is a clear vision of success, and the principal is able to*

articulate it in such a way that stakeholders understand the expectations and the outcomes.

Chapter 2

Learning the Lingo: Professional Development to Increase Student Growth

During the past twenty years, teacher professional development has transformed from a passive sit and listen model to an interactive, participatory, workshop model that stresses collaborative practices (Desimone & Garet, 2015). Coined by Mockler (in Loughran, 2014) 'spray-on professional development' has minimum short-term impact and no long-term impact (Loughran, 2014). Professional development is often top-down, content-focused, and chosen by leadership who believe they know best about what educators' need; rather, collaborative learning that is based on teachers' input, content-focused, and uses educator motivation as a facilitator of learning, is most successful.

As a seminal author, Knowles' (1984) theory of adult learning, or andragogy, can be stated using six assumptions related to the motivation to learn:

1. Need to know: Adults need to know the reason for learning something.
2. Foundation: Experience (including error) provides the basis for learning activities.
3. Self-concept: Adults must become self-directed, responsible for all educational decisions including the planning and evaluation of instruction.
4. Readiness: Adults are most interested in learning subjects having immediate relevance to their work and/or personal lives.
5. Orientation: Adult learning is problem-centered rather than content-oriented.
6. Motivation: Adults respond better to internal versus external motivators.

In accordance, successful features of andragogy reflect that teachers' autonomy is recognized in choosing their own content needs. Likewise, transformation leadership stresses working with teachers instead of directing them. Multiple studies show that the use of mentoring and coaching to understand content are vital to an effective PD plan (Desimone & Garet, 2015; Desimone & Pak, 2017).

Hall and Simeral (2017), discuss the need for a strong foundation that leads to student success. This is created when the building climate and culture shift, the faculty develop a reflective mindset, and a culture of reflective practice is established. To do this, several factors must be true throughout the building to include clarity of vision and goals, embracing change, open and transparent communication, continual progress towards group outcomes, and a culture that believes in deep reflection as a path to professional growth (Hall & Simeral, 2017).

It is this deep reflection that is the basis for an overall cultural shift. This shift is not created overnight; rather, it is an intentional and measured process that the principal and leadership team put into place through their own reflection and work in seven specific areas of change. Each provides the team with a piece of the larger puzzle to include (1) relationships, roles and responsibilities; (2) expectations and communication; (3) celebration and calibration; (4) goal setting and follow-through; (5) strategic PLC and teacher-leader teams; (6) transformational feedback; and (7) differentiated coaching (Hall & Simeral, 2017). In totality, these seven practices lead to how a culture of reflective practice is created and sustained.

A more formal practice, professional learning communities (PLCs) are comprised of teachers, specialists, and principals, and utilize new knowledge to teach content as well as "deepen understanding of how students learn content" (Bayar, 2014, p. 322). The complexity of the principal's role is to be more focused on his/her own qualities of leadership, how he/she understands the role in which they serve, and how the position has changed to meet the new demands (Zepeda, Parylo, & Bengtson, 2014).

The Principal's Role

As educators shift from individual focused professional development to that of collaboration with experiential learning, it quickly becomes imperative for the principal to have a well-designed plan (Desimone & Garet, 2015). The faculty assumes that the school leader is not only a learner in their own right but leads the march for cooperative learning among those who work in the school (Zepeda et al., 2014). Cooperative learning results in the development of a culture of collaborative learning; thus, improving both teaching practices and student learning (DuFour, DuFour, Eaker, & Mattos, 2016; Desimone & Garet, 2015).

As good as teacher development can be, however, most often forgotten is principal development. Principals as instructional leaders are expected to lead large groups of educators utilizing managerial skills, while creating conditions that encourage teachers' professional growth (Wallace Foundation, 2013; Zepeda et al., 2014). In the quest to improve student learning, a principal's "leadership is second only to classroom instruction" (Wallace Foundation, 2013, p. 5). Due to the lack of training on how to facilitate a learning community, many principals inadvertently use a deficit approach, which quickly becomes unsuccessful. Most principal development focuses on closing a gap in their knowledge; yet they need training to be able to help facilitate staff learning (Zepeda et al., 2014).

Leaders who have skills to guide teachers into the 21st century generally embody eight characteristics as defined by Matthews and Crow (in Zepeda et al., 2014). These include the roles of "a learner, a culture builder, an advocate, a leader, a mentor, a supervisor, a manager and a politician (p. 297). Principal preparation, however, is lacking in the andragogy that leads to effective instructional leadership, which often leads to attrition (Zepeda et al., 2014).

Principals are instructional leaders responsible for encouraging collaboration, communication, and shared responsibility among their educators and staff, while also addressing the daily administrative duties that tug for their attention (Fink, 2018). With this change in leadership focus comes the need to assess the "character development needed by leaders" (Turknett & Turknett, 2005, p. 1).

Referred to as the constructive theory of identity development, order of consciousness, or developmental theory, Kegan and Lahey (2009), proposed that andragogy is based on the idea that adults advance through five stages of development. Principals who want to make qualitative shifts in practice must first understand themselves and the work they are engaged in as well as how it relates to their staff, the school systems, and the world around them (Kegan & Lahey, 2009).

Thought of as starting during early development, a "child has not yet formulated the idea of a permanent, separate self" (Kegan & Lahey, 2016, p. 14). Most self-regulation behaviors are still in development during this period, and, as such, impulsiveness rules with little thought given regarding the ramifications of actions on others. In stage two, a young adolescence understands being different from another being; however, he or she is still very egocentric and is only able to understand his own perspective and not those around him (Kegan & Lahey, 2016).

Stage three appears in early adulthood and is demonstrated by those who are fully socialized, understand the perspective of others, look to others to help form their self-worth and value systems, and are trying different roles within a social context or are being instrumental in how they socialize with others (Kegan & Lahey, 2016). People in this stage are able to see different points of view and can sympathize and empathize with others, are responsible for relationships with others and avoid conflict, and are very aware of roles and responsibilities, and the effect on others (Kegan & Lahey, 2016).

Stage four is characterized by being self-authoring, having and sharing a value system and points of view that are specific to that particular person. The individual has acquired a worldview and "recognize[s] their own power in having done so" (Turknett & Turknett, 2005, p. 1). At this stage, there is an understanding of the power in personal feelings as well as the responsibility that comes with responses. People in this stage are able to deal with conflict and are not reliant on others. For principals this means being responsible and committed to the school or organization without being inundated by the amount of work to be done or the how others maybe reliant on them.

At stage four, adults are able to step back and outside of themselves to view their organization to make judgments, suggest changes that take into consideration the ramifications these decisions on others, understand how systems intertwine with one another, as well as the end result (Turknett & Turknett, 2005). Principals in this stage unearth talents in staff members not previously explored and cultivate a positive environment that fosters leadership qualities in others (Wallace Foundation, 2013).

In stage four, Kegan and Lahey (2016) would concede that the person is self-aware of personal ego; while at stage five is able to "expand their consciousness and move beyond their ego" (Turknett & Turknett, 2005, p. 2). Stage five, then, understands the "limits of their own value systems" (Turknett & Turknett, 2005, p. 1). Though people in this stage are able to hold conflicts at bay, they see, understand, and can explain larger systems (Kegan & Lahey, 2016). Adults are able to see the whole and parts, describing each separately and can explain and put the parts back into the whole again with changes in the systems being implemented.

Kegan and Lahey's (2016) theory makes a strong argument for how the developmental theory builds and maintains sustainability for professional leadership, nonetheless, years of data shows that "most adults in professional leaders' roles are primarily at stage three or between stages three and four, not stages four or five" (Turknett & Turknett, 2005, p. 2). This brings into question how professional development can become a training ground to foster the development of stronger stage four and emergent stage five leaders. Only 1% of the adult population ever make it to stage five, and with stage three having 58% and stage four 21% of the population; it is important that time and funds be targeted to building a larger cohort of principals who attain stage four (Turknett & Turknett, 2005; Kegan & Lahey, 2016). Wallace Foundation (2013) stresses that ongoing effective principal development that is strong in adult learning principles is crucial for leader preparation.

Mentoring and Coaching: Effective Professional Development

Though collaborative learning is preferred to build principal capacity, there are times when specific laser-like topics are focused on individual principal needs. In some cases, principal learning may be required to create instructional practices that can then transform teachers (Wallace Foundation, 2013; Zepeda et al., 2014). Principals should not lose sight of the need to provide adequate time to practice newly acquired skills, as well as reflection time, to staff as well as themselves. To sustain and extend learning, coaching and mentoring has become a valid method in the development of both principal and teacher capacity.

Positive evidence of job-embedded mentoring and coaching are viable ways to expand learning; rather than using workshop models according to Zepeda et al. (2014). Instructional coaching supports the development of teachers in evidence-based classroom practices through key features (Desimone & Pak, 2017). Coaching requires that content be the focus of the intervention and also that students engage actively in the learning. Coaching in this example gives the facilitator the opportunity to give feedback and to make suggestions for improved instruction (Desimone & Pak, 2017; Desimone & Garet, 2015).

Coaching brings coherence between the school's goals and curriculum, what teachers know and how the students learn it, through a deep understanding of needs (Desimone & Pak, 2017). This includes coaching for a long enough duration to change teacher pedagogy and through a community of practices (COP) or professional learning communities (PLC), where staff teaching similar content have adequate time to personalize and synthesize their instructional approaches (DuFour et al., 2016). Guided by principal leadership, these features of professional development make coaching an effective and potent part of a robust initiative that supports teachers (Desimone & Pak, 2017).

Teachers Coaching Teachers

The principals' time is well used in coaching, however, due to responsibility restraints professional development gained by having teachers coaching others or using instructional coaches is often more effective, especially if executed by a content-specialist. Based on the concepts of Vygotsky (1962), dialogue is critical to increasing personal knowledge. At its best, teachers who view themselves as life-long learners benefit immensely from coaching. Teachers, who are able to work in groups to refine practices, work collectively to amend ideas around culture and common core standards.

The role of the coach becomes that of a team leader with the purpose of keeping the group on track when teachers are on different levels of understanding content or have opposing views regarding student expectations. The principal should also be proficient in recognizing that differentiated instruction for the coaches may be necessary (DuFour et al., 2016). As the coaching team is formed, considerations around culture, beliefs, language differences, teacher perceptions and psychological orientations must be discussed (Haneda, Teemant & Sherman, 2017). "This results in four types of dialogue: inquiry (inclusive-convergent), conversation (inclusive-divergent), instruction (critical-convergent), and debate (critical-divergent)" (Haneda et al., 2017, p. 1749).

Coaches who used dialogue to stimulate inquiry and discovery by teachers were the most effective and aroused educator's knowledge of their own metacognition (Stahl, Sharplin, & Kehrwald, 2016). The use of small educator groups enabled the discussion of diverse perspectives and ideals, and included multiple cycles of feedback (Stahl et al., 2016). This type of coaching uses each teacher's Zone of Proximal Development or scaffolding to increase his or her teaching knowledge (Haneda et al., 2017).

A study by Pianta et al. (2017) examined the outcomes of combining master level coursework with intentional coaching around content using interventions taught in the course. The outcome of this study showed that coaches need to focus on the perceptions of participants regarding key aspects of interventions (Pianta, et al., 2017). In order for coaching to be effective, each principal needs to assess the developmental level of the teaching staff and what style of interventions will be most effective.

Data Teams and Professional Learning Communities

DuFour et al. (2016) posit that professional learning communities (PLC) are a valuable way to encourage collaboration among educators to solve critical learning issues facing diverse student populations. Using the PLC model, educators ask themselves four questions

- What do they want students to learn?
- How will they know when they have learned it?
- How do teachers respond to students who are not learning?

- How will instruction change when teachers realize that students know the information already?
(DuFour et al., 2016).

These guiding questions are beneficial for teachers to gather ideas on how their students are doing but do not furnish questions that help the teacher become data-informed nor do they always comprehend the purpose of the meeting. Integrating an effective team process for understanding how to use data to drive continuous improvement, Data Wise has improved instruction and learning in multiple school districts while building a culture of collaborative inquiry (Oberman & Boudett, 2015).

Teachers who use the PLC format and have a focused plan such as Data Wise to do a deep dig into the formative meaning of positive and negative data, are better prepared to validate findings, come to resolutions on negative data, and experience setting instructional strategies that are effective for all students (DuFour et al., 2016). Ferlazzo (2013) cites that focusing on being data-informed (rather that data-driven) is just one tool to use to create better learning plans for students. Teachers who use their knowledge of formative assessments, coupled with understanding student learning styles and other variables, can utilize and analyze data more efficiently and will be more appreciative of the challenges than statistics show (Oberman & Boudett, 2015).

Final Thoughts

Educator professional development has changed dramatically in recent history. No longer are teachers expected to take notes, internalize materials and spit them back out in an appropriate way to develop student's skills. The emphasis now is on interactive learning and coaching that are seen as premier ways to develop teaching pedagogy and a repertoire of interventions that benefit all students.

The principal, as instructional leader, has to understand the stages of personal consciousness in order to be able to provide support for the teachers. Principals who acknowledge their growth can assist in planning professional development that will be effective and beneficial for staff. Working in collaborative teams utilizing PLC's and frameworks such as Data Wise, school leaders and staff will see an increase in student learning and simultaneously realize teachers' professional growth in becoming data-informed decision makers (Boudett, City, & Murnane, 2017).

Points to Remember

- *Interactive, hands-on professional development is more effective than sit and listen workshops.*
- *Principals who recognize their won levels of development are consequential in helping design others' programs.*
- *Coaching, as an effective approach to professional development helps small groups of teachers learn both content and instructional strategies when led by an instructional coach.*
- *Instructional coaches that recognize the needs of groups of teachers can successfully plan interventions with staff that take into consideration cultural and knowledge perceptions.*
- *Coaches who utilize the Zone of Proximal Development (Vygotsky, 1962) help teachers become experts in their meta-cognition as they instruct their students.*
- *Using professional learning communities together with a data-informed framework such as Data Wise (Boudett et al., 2017) increases student learning.*

Chapter 3

Leveraging the Role of Teacher Unions: Striving for Collaboration and Mutual Respect

Teacher unions perform a variety of duties for teachers. They support professional development, provide legal help, and generally create better working conditions for teachers (Carini, 2002). The results of union activities are not only restricted to teacher working conditions, they also extend to students, who often perform higher academically than in schools without union support (Manzo, 2016; Vachon & Ma, 2015). Unions are not merely organizations that fight for their members, rather, they are touted to be actively involved with improving academic outcomes for students.

A positive partnership between teachers' unions and school administration benefits teachers and students alike (Rubinstein & McCarthy, 2014). Unions help in the generation of new data regarding best practices and help to disseminate information about those practices within the school district; therefore, the existence of unions is important to both students and teachers. The complex process of creating new working conditions and spreading information regarding best practices creates school environments staffed by well-paid educators who are knowledgeable in teaching. This has a considerable impact in the form of improved school performance (Vachon & Ma, 2015).

Union History

Unions provide many services to educators that often win them support and protect the rights and jobs of teachers (Carini, 2002). As early as 1857, unions fought to protect the rights of educators' who sought to express their opinions regarding the conditions of schools and tenure without fear of retaliation (Mader, 2012). In the 1930s, teachers were required to take loyalty oaths against communism and those with different viewpoints faced recrimination. This was one example of how unions fought for teachers' rights (Mader, 2012). Unions also fought to prevent teachers from being punished for their classroom management; such as furniture arrangements, lesson durations, and bulletin board formats. During the 1960s, union strikes were common due to teacher pay and school funding, while the 1970's federal court case of Abood v. Detroit stipulated that union dues to cover collective bargaining was constitutional, while collecting funds to cover political activities violated the First Amendment (Liptak, 2018). Since the beginning of the 21st century, recently unions have campaigned regarding teacher evaluations and merit pay (Mader, 2012).

Most recently, a complaint surfaced that mandatory union membership was illegal, which was in direct conflict with Abood v. Detroit. Specifically, the Janus Supreme Court Case "contends that because the activities of public unions are inherently political, being forced to support any portion of their [teachers] spending impinges on First Amendment rights" (Leef, 2018). Some educators, as well as other union-based workers, believe they should have the option to be part of the union, or not, and either way should not be penalized for that choice. The Janus decision was released on June 27, 2018, and it was determined that teachers who did not want to participate in the union would not be subject to pay dues (Liptak, 2018). This has the potential to change the very nature of how teachers are hired, retained, and supported.

Union Impact

Unions have similar impacts at the district, state, and national levels (Cowen & Strunk, 2015). Typically, unions at all levels engage in collective bargaining and political organizing. Collective bargaining is often the means by which unions wield their influence to negotiate for their members. This earns teachers increased benefits. For instance, public school teachers are often union members while private school teachers are not. Collective bargaining of the union is able to negotiate higher salaries for public school teachers, often up to 22% more than their private school peers; however, in exchange they often work longer days and have more advanced degrees (Manzo, 2016; DiCarlo, 2011).

National Level

Two primary, national teacher unions exist: The National Education Association (NEA) and the American Federation of Teachers (AFT). There are multiple benefits to joining these groups, such as incurring savings on different types of insurance, participation in discount programs, travel benefits, access to credit lines, opportunities to participate in education related activities, access to teacher-oriented publications, health club memberships, and legal services (Ravitch, n.d.).

The largest labor union in the country, the NEA represents 3.2 million public school teachers nationwide (Meador, 2017). This union recruits active and certified educators, school support staff, retired educators, and college students who plan to join the public school system as educators. The AFT has its roots in union work that dates back to 1916 (Carini, 2002). It represents 1.6 million members across the United States at every grade level. Similar to the National Education Association, the American Federation of Teachers protects both currently working and retired educators.

Occasionally, teachers do not agree with union politics. The National Education Association is often associated with supporting Democratic candidates, while the American Federation of Teachers is often associated with supporting Republican candidates. Teachers whose views run contrary to the candidates of either party, and the policies they support, may find themselves turned off from these groups (Meador, 2017; Singer, 2013). At the national level, unions wield political influence by helping to get representatives elected into Congress (Cowen & Strunk, 2015). Through the support of specific candidates, the hope is to elect individuals who will tout union-friendly causes. There is a clear advantage for teachers to benefit when unions advocate for certain candidates (Fagan, 2018).

Unions may have specific issues they fight against through the support of certain candidates, and these issues can range from merit pay to teacher evaluations (Fagan, 2018; Meador, 2017). In particular, the fight against the privatization of public schools has become one of the core battles that unions wage. These efforts hope to prevent legislation that would place corporations in charge of public school education, and teachers fear these companies are more concerned with turning profits than working on behalf of students.

Teachers often elect not to join a union for the financial reason of having to pay union dues or they do not agree that the work completed by unions merits membership (Meador, 2017). The combination of these issues ends with teachers shying away from joining a union; however, when membership is mandatory, educators must pay some portion of the dues (Meador, 2017). This is why the Janus decision will influence membership at a very basic level (Leef, 2018).

The impact of unions tends is also dependent on national contexts that impact how unions operate (Akiba & LeTendre, 2017). There are sometimes tensions between different stakeholders regarding the efforts of unions and these tensions are dissipated in countries that have an expectation of harmonious interactions between unions and schools, such as Sweden and Ireland.

Such expectations are not shared in countries such as the United States (Smith, 2015). In dialogue and narratives teachers are often framed as greedy, while children are often framed as victims. This narrative frame is used as an anti-union vehicle and drives resistance against teacher unions. Smith (2015) warned that teachers need to counter such assertions by recognizing their position in the public and creating narrative frames that emphasized the importance of children first rather than concepts such as the need for higher pay.

Still, prevalent anti-union rhetoric was reinforced by Akiba and LeTendre (2017) and Smith (2015), who noted that in some parts of the world there is greater tension and more frequent debate regarding the impact of teacher unions. When discussing the effectiveness and ability of a union to impact schools; therefore, it is important to consider the national conditions surrounding unions. Interactions between stakeholders vary from one nation to another.

Local Level

Unions exert influence at a local political level by supporting ballot initiatives that can enact union favored reforms (Cowen & Strunk, 2015). Teachers' unions are often favored by Democrats; thus, lobbying efforts tend to be lopsided with regard to which political party is supported in elections. Unions also manage to wield local political influence by lobbying for or against various policies considered by elected officials.

These union-led efforts may or may not support reforms, depending on whether the union considers the reform to be beneficial (Cowen & Strunk, 2015). On occasion, unions will attempt to undermine elements of a reform bill, like those requiring new methods of assessment, by drawing attention to the fallibilities of those assessments. At the local political level, unions exert power by influencing school board elections. This is an area where unions have a far more direct effect given the presence of teachers in the local community.

Teachers also exert significant influence at the local level by campaigning for the candidates they support and providing union endorsements for those individuals (Cowen & Strunk, 2015). This supports efforts to fundraise and mobilize voters in favor of these candidates. Union-endorsed candidates tend to win board seats at a disproportionate rate, indicating the influence that unions have at the local level (Singer, 2013). These candidates also tend to hold positions that favor the union, which favors the terms of teacher contracts signed. When school boards are staffed primarily by candidates who favor unions, teachers tend to win contracts that favor themselves, rather than the best interests of students or the school administration (Singer, 2013).

Professional Development

Unions help in the professional development of teachers by providing both state specific and nationwide training opportunities that offer teachers a chance to develop professionally (Bangs & MacBeth, 2012). By providing staff support assistance, mentorship training, and leadership training, unions give teachers a chance to grow professionally in a number of ways (Illinois Federation of Teachers, 2018).

Local unions often host national conferences where teachers can engage with one another and receive additional training (Bangs & MacBeth, 2012). Teachers not only connect with one another, but they also connect with researchers. As part of this networking, teachers learn to devise ways of promoting education and various teaching approaches. Unions also support teacher development through workshops, online sessions, and by providing teaching strategy tools (Illinois Federation of Teachers, 2018).

The efforts at the school and district level are supported at the state level through the development of institutions that offer leadership and skill training (Rubinstein & McCarthy, 2014). This training helps support lower level efforts, resulting in teachers who benefit from professional networks, new knowledge, and greater training. From a research perspective, efforts from the state to the local level can be supplemented by convening conferences designed to examine best practices (Rubinstein & McCarthy, 2014). These conventions focus discussions around the best approaches toward instruction and means by which collaboration can improve school performance. Conferences also afford opportunities for schools to receive technical support in implementing new practices.

Independent of conferences, research should be ongoing on collaborative school reform efforts. Research shows these efforts are connected with improved school performance, and should continue (Rubinstein & McCarthy, 2014). This research supports schools throughout the districts in the same way that conferences spread the use of specific best practices across districts (Rubinstein & McCarthy, 2014). Union activity results in the enforcement of rigorous credentialing processes (Vachon & Ma, 2015). Unions, therefore, ensure there are more thoroughly trained teachers in the classroom, resulting in a greater level of security for teachers, which may add to their performance in positive ways.

Impact on Students

Teachers unions are associated with improved academic performance among students (Vachon & Ma, 2015). There are differences in test scores and graduation rates among schools with a unionized teaching force, versus those without such a base (Manzo, 2016). Compared to non-unionized members, for example, teachers who are union members are 16 percent more likely to have advanced degrees and higher skill abilities (Manzo, 2016).

Unions may help to improve working conditions, leading to a number of factors that benefit teachers, such as higher pay (Manzo, 2016). Regardless of the specific benefits that unions achieve for their members, they create better working conditions overall, and this is associated with a positive effect on student performance. It is important to look at unions internationally in order to understand how they affect student performance. The countries with the strongest teacher unions also have some of the best student performance, while there is minimal evidence that unions have a negative impact on student outcomes (Cowen & Strunk, 2015; Manzo, 2016, Ravini, 2014).

While the international effect was not studied to determine a specific correlation, it anecdotally provided some support for the idea that unions help to provide the conditions that create improved student performance (Cowen & Strunk, 2015). Within the United States, those states with the strongest union participation included Alaska, with over 67 percent participation; and New York, Rhode Island, New Jersey, Maine, and Illinois all with participation rates between 63 and 54 percent (Manzo, 2016). These states with high levels of membership were able to use the influence of teachers on state education decisions, allowed teachers to strike, and mobilized teachers to vote for supportive political candidates (DiCarlo, 2011).

The existing research reviewed by Vachon and Ma (2015) on the impact of teacher unions indicate they have a positive influence on student achievement. These unions are involved in policymaking, bringing valuable experience to the shaping of policies that are best suited to guiding the instruction of students. Teachers advocate for their students and help to shape the policies best suited to them. These enhance teaching quality and improve student achievement, making unions an important part of giving teachers a voice in the policy making process.

Baron (2018) also suggested that unions have a positive influence on student performance. The study was conducted in response to the Budget Repair Bill enacted in Wisconsin, which served to limit the power of teacher unions, restricted the unions' ability to fundraise, and limited the extent to which they could become involved in collective bargaining (Baron, 2018). Baron (2018) examined the timing of the budget repair bill and the performance of students on state standardized exams and determined that the law reduced the average test scores on standardized exams by approximately 20% of a standard deviation (Baron, 2018). The drop-in performance was particularly significant among students already on the lower end of student achievement distribution, compounding the already existing poor performance within that group (Baron, 2018).

To assess the impact of unions on school performance, data was drawn from California to assess the relationship between the two (Wydra, 2018). The performance of students at unionized California charter schools was compared using data from California Standards Tests. Forty-six schools were selected for final inclusion in the study. These schools often experienced a change in union status during their existence, allowing researchers to examine how student achievement was impacted with and without unions present (Wydra, 2018).

The comparisons demonstrated that school in which there were active unions student performance in math increased (Wydra, 2018). A positive impact of about .17 standard deviations was detected, making the improvements statistically significant (Wydra, 2018). The researchers contextualized the study, noting that separate research they reviewed indicated the unions might only affect specific subsets of the student population.

The findings were similar to that of Vachon and Ma (2015), who found that mid and high achieving students were most impacted in schools with active unions. Within the context of the study, Wydra (2018) found those most affected by active unions were low performing students. This contrast demonstrates that the impact of unions is different in different contexts.

There is evidence that the impact of teacher unions may not always be positive (Strunk & McEachin, 2011). Research in California centered on the relationship between collective bargaining agreements negotiated by unions and school district performance. The researchers used California's state standards as the baseline for determining how the union impacted outcomes (Strunk & McEachin, 2011). At the conclusion of the study, it was found that collective bargaining agreements that were particularly restrictive often negatively impacted schools (Strunk & McEachin, 2011).

Schools dealing with the restrictions placed on them by one of these agreements were more likely to be in a program improvement phase as well as to have both lower proficiency and graduation rates (Strunk & McEachin, 2011). This effect was magnified when the school or district had a high proportion of minority, low income, and low achieving students. This evidence suggested that restrictive contracts negatively impacted performance (Strunk & McEachin, 2011).

Strunk (2011) offered a counterpoint to the findings found by Strunk and McEachin (2011) and suggested that collective bargaining agreements had led to increased school spending; however, this spending did not go toward book, supplies, and school related expenditures, rather, it went toward paying more to administrators or instruction related spending. How money was spent, rather than the simple state of increased spending, may have been to blame for decreased performance in schools dealing with restrictive contracts.

Despite the findings by Strunk (2011), Lott & Kenny (2013) found evidence to support the notion that teacher unions negatively impacted outcomes. The researchers specifically examined district union strength and their financial resources; that is, both union dues per teacher and union expenditures per student were examined. At the conclusion of the study, Lott & Kenny (2013) found that students in states with strong state-wide teacher unions had lower proficiency rates when compared to students in states with weak state-wide teacher unions. Student test scores were lower in states where teacher unions collected greater union dues (Lott & Kenny, 2013). These findings indicated that unions may have a negative impact on student outcomes.

Part of the reason that negative outcomes have been found in states with strong teacher unions may be due to the lower staffing ratios that unions are willing to accept (Brunner & Squires, 2013). Lower student to teacher ratios are typically associated with improved student outcomes; however, strong unions often negotiate for increased returns to teacher seniority and are willing to sacrifice both base teacher salaries and staffing ratios (Brunner & Squires, 2013). This leaves much of the teaching staff both underpaid and overworked. Only the most senior of teachers' experience greater pay at the expense of pay to novice teachers.

Partnerships that Enhance Student Outcomes

Blame is often placed on teachers for low student achievement; however, there are larger system issues facing students that include poverty, systemic racism, and income inequality (Strauss, 2016). There should be appropriate methods for assessing teacher quality; yet the methods for assessment are often lackluster, and questions persist regarding the accuracy of these assessments.

Many assessments lack the ability to show the effort that teachers put into improving student confidence and attitudes toward learning (Strauss, 2016). These improvements in attitude lead to improved academic success and yet are not integrated into teacher assessments. Other variables that affect teacher performance include socioeconomic status, gender, ethnicity, education level, and race (Strauss, 2016). Often, these considerations are not taken into account when assessing teachers and their instructional quality; thus, teaching assessments continue to be incomplete.

In general, testing seems to be the only adequate means of informing student achievement (Rubinstein & McCarthy, 2014). Testing can help identify difficulties among students, but the benefits do not extend much beyond that. To build on the results generated by tests, union-management partnerships can help drive new student learning. Union-management partnerships encourage collaboration between educators as well as the conceptualization of new solutions to difficulties in student achievement (Rubinstein & McCarthy, 2014).

Partnerships bring key stakeholders together in order to encourage the student improvement process; yet there are few examples of how such partnerships have produced improvements that benefited students (Rubinstein & McCarthy, 2014). The creation of formal partnerships that unite the unions, administrators, and teachers at the local school level is associated with improved student performance after taking into account the school type and poverty level. These partnerships can be accomplished in two primary ways.

Partnerships created extensive communication between teachers (Rubinstein & McCarthy, 2014). When higher quality teacher-administrator partnerships were encouraged, increased collaboration arose between those participating in the relationship (Rubinstein & McCarthy, 2014). Communication regarding student performance, curriculum development, cross-subject integration, and sharing new instructional practices all contributed to the performance of students (Rubinstein & McCarthy, 2014). These partnerships also afforded teachers a greater chance to receive mentoring that benefited those instructors.

Partnerships also helped to improve communication regarding student performance (Rubinstein & McCarthy, 2014). Discussions surrounding student performance data, curriculum integration, and instructional practice were all improved and resulted in increased student performance (Rubinstein & McCarthy, 2014). The degree of communication also increased and became less formal between union representatives and principals. As union representatives and principals worked together, conditions also improved for teachers (Rubinstein & McCarthy, 2014).

Union-management partnerships contribute to improved performance within a school by creating a more positive climate where teacher collaboration and innovation are encouraged, and infrastructure is improved (Rubinstein & McCarthy, 2014). Traditionally, collaboration is a means of encouraging improved student achievement, demonstrating the value that union-management partnerships have on public schools. These incentives encourage the creation of union-management partnerships and collaboration (Rubinstein & McCarthy, 2014). These same incentives can encourage improved curriculum performance, improved instructional practice, better teacher evaluations, more professional development, and both mentoring and peer review (Rubinstein & McCarthy, 2014).

Another way these partnerships can be encouraged is by providing both technical and financial support to school districts that demonstrate a willingness to pilot innovative and collaborative approaches to improving instructional delivery in an attempt to improve student performance (Rubinstein & McCarthy, 2014). Within those districts, educators should be allowed a chance to build networks and link the experiences of these individuals. Encouraging increased networks between these individuals encourages collaboration (Rubinstein & McCarthy, 2014). In particular, teachers from inexperienced districts benefit as they encounter new best practices for instructional delivery and acquire new support for their own efforts.

Final Thoughts

Teacher unions have the potential to help create positive work environments and encourage professional development that supports improved instructional methods (Meador, 2017; Manzo, 2016; Baron, 2018; Ravani, 2014). When unions coordinate with schools, there are positive outcomes for both students and teachers, with improved academic performance and instructional methods observed (Rubinstein & McCarthy, 2014; Vachon & Ma, 2015). Yet negative impacts do exist when unions, teachers, and administration do not see eye-to-eye or when the union pushes for mandates and candidates that are not on pace with member and non-members beliefs. It is important, then, to be cautiously optimistic and work with unions to advance school doctrine and improve student outcomes.

Points to Remember

- *History has proven that unions can be powerful machines that can help or hinder academic progress. It is up to the members and administration to push for initiatives that improve outcomes.*

- *In schools where unions have higher membership, students appear to have better test scores and higher graduation rates. Union members tend to have higher wages; however, they also have advanced educational degrees and work longer hours.*

- *Union members may be able to take advantage of more professional development although in the past this has meant being out of the building at conferences; thus, teachers are forced to produce lesson plans and students often receive sub-par teaching during this time.*

- *The Janus decision has completely upended unions and membership dues. As such, unions will have to reconfigure their organizations and teachers may find they have fewer benefits as well as being at the mercy of administration with little, if any, job security.*

Chapter 4

Goal Setting to Raise the Bar: Improving the School from Within

Schoolwide goal setting is an effective tool to ensure higher levels of student achievement. Principals who have high standards guide teachers in planning their goals and "to ensure their teaching and learning activities are effectively executed (Bakar, Yun, Keow, & Li, 2014, p. 41). Often completed with the assistance of a school leadership team, schoolwide goal setting is often designed at the beginning of the year following student testing and subsequent data assimilation and using common core standards that are grade appropriate. When principals understand goal-setting theory, they are better prepared to support teachers, set student achievement goals, as well as the strategies that go with them (Bakar et al., 2014).

The Elementary and Secondary Education Act (ESSA) requires that all schools and districts have improvement plans that cover content areas, parent-school partnerships, attendance, and discipline (Samuels, 2016). ESSA is part of a long heritage of school reforms that are aimed at improving students' scores, ensuring that all students have college and career readiness skills, and are ready for life beyond high school (Samuels, 2016). ESSA's predecessor, the No Child Left Behind Act (NCLB) and Race to the Top required that all efforts include research-based strategies; however, "both of these reform initiatives largely ignored specific practices ground in research" (DuFour & Mattos, 2013, p. 35).

NCLB and Race to the Top were based on coupling teacher evaluation with student scores (Klein, 2016). This approach did nothing to enhance schools; rather, it compromised teacher confidence, diminished the focus on student learner concepts, as well as the bigger picture of school improvement that led to student achievement (DuFour & Mattos, 2013). Under ESSA, strategies put into place must be evidence based and, theoretically, improve practices through "collective analysis of evidence of student learning" (DuFour & Mattos, 2013, p. 35). ESSA encouraged principals to leverage personal and school teams' knowledge, as well as that of others (families and stakeholders) to create school level educational models that were well-rounded (Center on Great Teachers and Leaders at American Institutes for Research, 2017).

As a result of past legislative approaches, it was decided that the most effective way to increase student achievement was not only to focus on student successes but also to include changes in three other categories to include school environment and climate, changing demographics, and implementation (Center on Great Teachers and Leaders at American Institutes for Research, 2017). Student learning considers curriculum transfer, assessments, whole child learning including social and emotional domains, and tests. School environment includes how families and students feel connected to their school community and to one another in the school, what the climate or environment within the school is, and families' perceptions of the school. Lastly, the demographics consider changing student populations with an increase of students of color, poverty rates, students identified with special learning needs and sexual orientation, gender and race.

Goal Setting Theory of Motivation

Originally defined by Edwin Locke in the 1960s, the goal setting theory stated that clearly defined, realistic goals that were challenging and attainable in nature, increased the motivation of those who were required to complete a task (Locke & Latham, 1990). Five principles worked together to improve the success rate of the individual involved in task completion to include clarity, challenge, commitment, feedback, and task complexity (Locke & Latham (1990). The theory maintained that higher levels of self-confidence would lead to task completion and feelings of accomplishment; conversely, low levels of confidence would lead to task failure and frustration. The original tenets put forth by Locke & Latham (1990), served as the basis for creating SMART goals.

Developing SMART Goals

Utilizing a method called SMART enables schools to have a comprehensive system in place to implement and measure goals with specific end dates. SMART stands for specific, measurable, appropriate, realistic, and time limited (Wesolowski, 2015). From the creation of SMART goals, instructional strategies and action steps are developed. Also included in the goals are communication strategies to guide stakeholders as well as the professional development staff will need to become exemplary teachers who can lead students to academic success (Wesolowski, 2015). Goal areas targeted in the School Improvement Plan (SIP) include content areas of literacy and numeracy, school climate, parent/family engagement, discipline and attendance (Hanover Research, 2014). SMART objectives are used to inform instructional practices that are effective and measurable (Wesolowski, 2015).

School goals should not look like a 'to do' list; rather, they should begin with action words (verbs) that drive the school towards achievement (Barile, 2015). Words such as plan, research, mandate, increase, design, focus, or implement all implies action (Barile, 2015). Action plans should strategically include both big picture items and an eye for breaking larger tasks into smaller parts. Effective plans become systemic and sustainable (Sparks, 2018). Using a planning team with both skills will be valuable to the planning process and will help individuals connect the plan specifics to the overarching goals of the school district such as coherence plans (Barile, 2015).

Short-term goals incrementally lead to long-term goals; therefore, it is important for principals to consider appropriate short-term goals that are built in to accomplish the more difficult long-term ones (Bakar et al., 2014). Goal composition is important when considering how goals are formed. Goals that are set too high often result in improvement plans that never come to fruition; however, goals that are set too low will never see the return on tasks that are expected. Finding a middle ground that both excites and motivates staff is paramount to seeing outcome success in improvement plans (Hanover Research, 2014).

Wesolowski (2015) posits that there are three different types of goals when considering in planning; those of global, educational, and instructional. The different types of goals vary in specificity and are customary in educational theory (Wesolowski, 2015). Global objectives are wide-ranging and can encompass a myriad of goals; educational objectives are wide-ranging and often called long-term goals; whereas, instructional objectives are very specific and are developed by teachers for the learning needs of the children in the classrooms. Global and educational objectives are most likely put into place using a team approach comprised of school leadership, data teams and other engaged in student learning (Wesolowski, 2015).

Many schools may find that at vital points during the planning process outside help is needed from a consultant or someone higher in the district administration to assist the team in staying focused and lessen frustration. It is necessary to ensure the team has the time to stop and assess both the goals and the progress, and that there are benchmark points built into the action plans to document successes (Education Trust, n.d.). The action plan timeline must be both realistic and obtainable. It is imperative that teams take the time to thoroughly reflect on the proposed changes and are prepared to find obstacles or barriers that may affect the original timeline (Education Trust, n.d.). Though action plans may be going smoothly, in most cases, there will be room for improvement that can be brought forward by outside stakeholders and others not intimately associated to the plan (Hanover Research, 2014).

Designing School Improvement Plans

Educational institutions have been sluggish in considering continuous improvement as a way to increase student achievement; rather, schools employed multiple teaching strategies that were implemented with little results (Hanover Research, 2014). The Elementary and Secondary Education Act requires that all school have improvement plans designed by a team led by the principal or school leadership (Hanover Research, 2014). Most principals assemble a teacher from each grade, or department chairs, content specialist, data specialists, and others with knowledge of how the school functions that may include families and key stakeholders. School improvement plans normally have a theory of action that leads principals to tailor individual school goals based on multiple factors (Center for Educational Leadership, 2014).

Theory of action statements are a hypothesized sequence of events that can be used to develop individual goals (Center for Educational Leadership, 2014). An example of an overarching statement from which a plan would be created might be "If we ensure that every lesson is planned using standards-based curricula, is rigorous and is taught in a differentiated manner designed to meet the learning needs of each student, then we will accelerate learning and close the identified achievement gaps" (Danbury Public Schools, 2011, n.p.). Most districts have these overarching theory of action statements, which are significant in driving individual schools improvement plans (Center for Educational Leadership, 2014).

SIPs are designed after careful and comprehensive assessment of high need areas, student learning needs, level of family engagement, and other data such as attendance, truancy, and discipline (Hanover Research, 2014). School Improvement plans are comparable to "a road map that sets out the changes a school need to make to improve the level of student achievement and shows how and when these changes will be made" (Hanover Research, 2014, p. 18). Improvement plans become the living document that schools will utilize to ensure student success and as part of the ESSA requirement to use evidence-based strategies (Education Trust, n.d.; Klein, 2016).

The SIP identifies problems of practice or the root cause of disparities that form the baseline for designing the plan. Many schools consider the baseline assessment to be what schools are currently doing or their performance, and then plan for the change they expect (Hanover Research, 2014). Baseline data that includes both quantitative and qualitative data coupled with a list of priorities form the next stage in the plan (Hanover Research, 2014). Principals must then examine the needs of the school and the data supplied to create two to five priorities. Priorities that are lengthy and ill-focused will cause undue stress and divert the team away from critical needs; therefore, developing a list of high-needs and high impact areas will make the process manageable and efficacious (Hanover Research, 2014).

Several needs assessments are readily available at this stage in the development of the plan. Cambridge Education, the Association for Supervision and Curriculum Development, the National Association of Elementary Principals, and Six Sigma have plans that are readily available on the Internet (Hanover Research, 2014). Some districts bring in consultants to lead groups through this process, which is especially helpful with novice principals. Consultants are valuable when large districts undertake improvement planning. Instead of higher-level management trying to coordinate efforts, determine similarities between schools, as well as what valuable resources each school has available, the consultant is given this role of synchronization; especially where coherence between schools is important (Hanover Research, 2014; Sparks, 2018).

Developing Appropriate Measures and Tracking Growth

All schools and classrooms that have goals in place should have measures, or metrics, that will be used for assessment built into place during the planning stage. In many cases, it is easier to use backwards design, a concept in which school leaders and educators begin with the end in mind (Hanover Research, 2014; Wiggins & McTighe, 2017). This three-part process includes identifying desired outcomes, identifying acceptable evidence, and planning the experiences and instruction that will lead to the predetermined outcomes (Wiggins & McTighe, 2017).

When using the SMART goals, technique, measurement, and time limited strategies are built into the process. Deciding what the measurement will be in the planning process gives the school benchmarks along the process to monitor (Wesolowski, 2015). Many different tools can be used to track the effectiveness of the strategy. Effective tools include anecdotal records, computer spreadsheets, formal measurement programs, and benchmarks.

Schools may develop a task-referential orientation where the focus is on the completion of the job recognized by the person charged with accomplishing the goal; whereas, the performance goal orientation focuses on the planned outcomes and is recognized by others, feedback, and by the individual who planned the goal, in this case, it may be the principal (Bakar et al., 2014). It is a fine line that determines which method works best. It is easy to underperform or overperform depending on the person leading the tasks; regardless, the purpose of school improvement plans is to see increased student scores. Who decides which method is used or how they are obtained is usually left for the individual person delegated to meet the goal targets; this is usually the school leader and staff (Hanover Research, 2014).

Written into school improvement plans should be a way to track growth over time. A timeline should be structured into the plan that follows the school year calendar. Expecting staff to be able to devote time to accomplishing goals over the summer break is both unrealistic and for many outside their contracts (U.S. Department of Education, 2014). Many districts and schools go through the planning stage in the spring with the expectation that working on the actual goals will begin at the start of the school year. A full year to implement the plan provides enough time for a comprehensive change and quantifiable outcomes (Hanover Research, 2014).

In many cases when new learning programs or novel strategies are executed there is often an implementation gap or dip. This dip is most likely attributed to the time it takes a new program to be thoroughly implemented, or the time it takes to move from one style of performing a task to the new initiative (Bakar et al., 2014). Research shows that the best way to reverse implementation gaps are for principals to directly work with teachers to ensure their classroom goals are aligned with the overarching school objectives (Hanover Research, 2014).

Principals Helping Teachers to Set Classroom Goals

To ensure that educators are serving all children appropriately in a cycle of academic improvement, many schools have adopted Data Wise, which uses cyclical and collaborative data inquiry to drive improvement of teaching strategies and student achievement (Boudett et al., 2017). Another effective way to encourage teachers to set goals aligned with the overarching school goals is to use TARGET (Bakar et al., 2014). Similar to other goal setting strategies, schoolwide teacher professional development is usually required to understand TARGET as the process must be internalized and synthesized by staff prior to implementation (Bakar et al., 2014). This method includes six dimensions to be used in succession and include task design, distribution of authority, recognition of pupils, grouping arrangements, evaluation practices, and time allocation.

- Task Design: As teachers begin to design the first dimension, the goal should be focused on challenging the abilities of the student in multiple ways, using sensory and experiential strategies and "where students can complete tasks with guidance" (Bakar et al., 2014, p. 44).
- Distribution of Authority: The second dimension of planning considers how students can be engaged in the planning process (Bakar et al., 2014). Student-centered learning engages teams of students and

teachers in robust experiences that enhance intrinsic motivation through personal choice regarding individual educational paths (Spangler et al., 2016). This focuses students on their own sense of control and responsibility as well as helps them set personal short and long-term goals (Bakar et al., 2014).

- Recognition of Pupils: The recognition of students through strategic and personal feedback shared mutually between the student and teacher is the focus of the third dimension. Personal motivation to complete tasks increases due to feedback that recognizes the accomplishments of the student; in turn, mastery of content occurs (Bakar et al., 2014).

- Group Arrangements: This dimension considers the classroom climate where students have the ability to work individually or in mixed groups (Bakar et al., 2014). Through teacher observation students are placed into groups that scaffold their abilities and knowledge. Groups can also observe one another and make suggestions for learning opportunities that help excel the students in the sixth dimension of evaluation.

- Evaluation Practices: Evaluation can take place individually or within groups using predetermined metrics. In most cases, it is when students have acquired the skills necessary to be considered competent in a subject area and "students move ahead as they demonstrate mastery" (Spangler et al., 2016).

- Time Allocation: Quality student-centered learning gives pupils time to move at a pace that helps refine their skills through experiences that they take the time to design and implement. (Spangler et al., 2016). Teachers can help by suggesting alternative strategies and adjustments to timelines when needed (Bakar et al., 2014).

- Regardless of the specific goal setting method used, it is vital to take district goals and drill them down to the school and then classroom level as a means to improve student achievement of all students.

Final Thoughts

The leadership team, in conjunction with the principal, is responsible for creating goals that align with both the district and school mission and take into account the needs of the student population before them. These goals become the school improvement plan, which is then further funneled to create educator and classroom goals. Using a variety of strategies to ensure the goals have all the necessary ingredients ensures that students receive high quality education. School improvement depends on all stakeholders working to first define, then create, and finally implement goals that meet the requirements of the district, the school, and the needs of all students.

Points to Remember

- *Goal setting is an effective tool to increase positive student outcomes. At the school level, a leadership team is usually responsible for working with the principal to determine specific school needs and subsequent goals as a means to reach higher levels of student achievement.*

- *Federal policies prescribe the use of district and schoolwide measures to gauge student achievement to include student learning, school culture and climate, demographics, and the school improvement plan implementation, to name a few.*

- *The school improvement plan (SIP) is written by the leadership team based on district-wide goals that are brought down to the school level. Overarching statements become more focused goals and have a direct and intentional impact on student learning.*

- *SMART goals enable schools to have a comprehensive system in place to define, implement, and measure specific goals. These strategic goals must be reasonable and attainable.*

- *TARGET is another system that principals can implement at the educator level where six dimensions are completed in sequential order. This system can piggyback on the SMART goals and the SIP as a way to ensure an alignment of schoolwide goals.*

Chapter 5

The Critical Nature of Data Driven Decision Making: Improving Academic Performance through Analytics

Due in part to legislative accountability standards, principals often adopt data driven decision making to improve educator performance and student outcomes (Siemens & Baker, 2012). Principals generally use individual and aggregate teacher and student performance data to set goals (Sun, Johnson, & Przybylski, 2016). While there is a lack of consensus among researchers and practitioners regarding how to use students' academic performance data to improve outcomes, scholarly research indicates that including teachers in the process of setting data-based goals improves outcomes (Sun et al., 2016). Principals who include faculty in the process of setting teaching and learning goals based on data analysis results are more likely to see improved student academic performance (Sun et al., 2016).

Defining Data Driven Decision-Making

Simply put, data driven decision-making refers to intentional and repetitive conversations between school leaders and educators surrounding statistics as a means to improve teaching and learning (Boudett et al., 2017). This cyclical collaboration becomes the catalyst for change; enhancing all aspects of the school including educator teaching practices, student outcomes, and building-wide culture and climate (Boudett et al., 2017).

The urgency with which schools have attempted to implement more specific data driven decision-making methods has been due to the need to meet federal standards, such as those placed by the former federal No Child Left Behind Act (Marsh, Pane, & Hamilton, 2006). Such laws place downward pressure on schools to draw upon data in ways that can improve test scores. A great deal of variety exists in how leaders conceptualized the process as well as how data impacts decisions involving the use of resources at the district and school levels (Marsh et al., 2006; Ikemoto & Marsh, 2007).

In a 2007 study by Ikemoto and Marsh, it was discovered that decision-making at all levels, from the classroom to the district level, were impacted by different forms of data. Different levels of the education system prioritized different forms of data. At the educator level, for example, assessment results were used to make straightforward decisions on differentiated instruction to mitigate gaps in learning, while others created action plans to address whole class needs (Ikemoto & Marsh, 2007). The results highlighted how data is prioritized differently at all tiers of the education system; yet the results also demonstrated how data drove decision-making (Ikemoto & Marsh, 2007).

There has been a rise in the demand for data and analytics to improve the learning process (Siemens & Baker, 2012). As data collection has developed, increasingly large volumes of data sets have become available that can be drawn upon for informing the educational process. This has partly been the result of student engagement with educational software and online learning applications that collects and analyzes data behind the scenes and gives it to educators in an easy to understand manner (Siemens & Baker, 2012). In response, organizations have coalesced around the concept of creating a higher quality analysis of large education-based data sets (Siemens & Baker, 2012). The sheer volume of data available, however, is indicative of the degree to which data is potentially available to administrators, making it necessary that school leaders be well versed in how to make decisions based on the available data.

The appropriate use of data in the decision-making process holds the potential to increase student performance (Wohlstetter, Datnow, & Park, 2008). The data collected within a school can be used to determine where the school stands in comparison to district and state standards as well as to improve the school's performance by examining the efficacy of existing curriculum and teaching practices (Wholstetter et al., 2008). The end benefits of these changes are about more than just improving school performance; rather, data-informed decisions address the moral need to ensure that equitable opportunities for all students exist (Datnow, 2017).

The appropriate use of data can help provide relatively equitable outcomes even among diverse populations within a school that traditionally underperform. The main barrier to this outcome is that principals and teachers often do not understand how to properly address the data that they have at hand; yet when properly implemented, data-informed decisions open the door to improved achievement for all students (Datnow, 2017).

Decision-Making Systems

Improving educational instruction using data requires the appropriate systems to support the generation of data (Wohlstetter et al., 2008; Halverson, 2010). Principals play a key role in determining the systems by which data is acquired and analyzed in order to meet federal goals. Once implemented, the systems have to support the interpretation of data so that appropriate changes in instruction can be made (Halverson, 2010). Even when data is available, there are limits to whether it can be implemented effectively (Wohlstetter et al., 2008). A system must be in place to aligns goals at multiple levels, from the district to the classroom level. No part of the educational process can be considered entirely independent of the rest. When it comes to setting school level goals, they should align upward to the district level.

The data that districts use to inform their standards relies on organization level statistical collection. Data can be generated at the classroom level using a formative feedback system, which can guide the teaching process (Boudett et al., 2017; Halverson, 2010). Although formative feedback systems were originally conceptualized as a means of gaining insight into results at the classroom level; they can also be extended to the entire organization (Halverson, 2010). Researchers proposed that this method of data driven decision-making relies on a three-function process that includes introducing interventions to guide learning, taking assessments to gauge the success of interventions, and an actuation stage in which school staff learn from those assessments and alter how their programs are structured (Halverson, 2010).

In order to make appropriate decisions regarding the education process, the data generated must illustrate the outcomes of various instructional methods. The data collected during assessments should be brought together by faculty, meeting as a group, to review outcomes and determine ways in which the education process can be improved (Boudett et al., 2017; Halverson, 2010). Data generated at the classroom level informs changes to instructional delivery and, in some occasions, wholesale changes to the interventions being used in the classroom (Datnow, 2017).

Faculty meetings, or PLCs, take on great importance when a formative feedback system is in place, as they provide the time for reflection and improvement of existing education systems (Halverson, 2010). Formative assessment data has also been used to help improve equitable outcomes among students (Datnow, 2017). By closely examining student and assessment outcomes, teachers are able to differentiate instruction to target areas where each specific student is weak, such as in areas of fluency or mathematical reasoning. Nuanced understandings of what students are capable of allow for more targeted instruction. This requires that assessments be used to inform instructional changes that address each student's specific areas of weakness (Boudett et al., 2017).

Levels of Decision-Making

At the school level, administrators should evaluate where their schools currently stand and establish future directions for their organizations (Wohlstetter et al., 2008). Consistent with the need for goals to be aligned, schools should implement instructional guidelines based on state standards, for example. From the state to the district and the school, the overall goals should be aligned, yet administrators should allow teachers flexibility in the classroom to teach to the needs of their class. This type of aligned system allows for top-down guidance of classroom activity while allowing bottom-up flexibility in practice among teachers (Wohlstetter et al., 2008).

Administrators sit somewhere in between the classroom level and the district level. Though not responsible for classroom level decisions on a day-to-day basis, they are also not responsible for establishing the organization-wide goals that districts place upon individual schools. Those goals guide the actions schools take and influence what happens within the classroom.

In practice, many models of data driven decision-making in schools are derived from other industries (Marsh et al., 2006). Processes like Total Quality Management and Continuous Improvement place an emphasis on data driven improvements at the organizational level (Murray, 2017). Administrators most commonly rely on student outcome data as such data follows assessments of student knowledge across a range of academic skills. School principals rely on these in many cases when making decisions regarding changes to organizational behavior and view such data as useful in the data-making process (Marsh et al., 2006).

One issue with student outcome data is that it is summative and only puts forward statistical information from a brief moment in time (Marsh et al., 2006). Value added modeling is one proposed way of increasing the value of data (Koedel, Mihaly, & Rockoff, 2015). Such models control for various factors to identify specifically how schools contribute to a student's performance rather than outside factors, such as family background (Koedel et al., 2015). Administrators, however, seem to be rarely aware of value added models and how the data generated from such models can contribute to an understanding of a school's performance. Consequently, school administrators become reliant on summative data from tests to inform their perception of their school's performance (Marsh et al., 2006). In many cases, test results are made available too late in the year to make adjustments and address school performance.

The most common summative tests used to help schools understand how they are performing against standards, students, and districts are often distributed in the spring and many times the results are not released back to the schools until the end of the year or over the summer (Marsh et al., 2006). As a result, the data drawn from the tests is of limited use. The tested population has, by that time, progressed onward a grade level, moved into different classes, or even moved on to different schools. In response to this, schools have adopted more frequent tests taken throughout the year that make it possible to gauge how the school is performing with enough time to be actionable (Achievement Network, n.d.; Bill & Melinda Gates Foundation, 2015).

School principals and administrators seem to consider more frequent tests performed at the school level as a force for improving their schools (Bill & Melinda Gates Foundation, 2015). In comparison to state mandated testing, these local level tests can be conducted more frequently, and the results made available almost immediately for making changes to school goals, instructional methods, and student interventions (Achievement Network, n.d.; Bill & Melinda Gates Foundation, 2015). Other types of frequent data that can inform changes to instructional methods include daily reflections and educator notes, exit tickets, and classroom discussions (Edutopia, 2015). While school-wide, frequent testing is beneficial to administrators, teachers can also use these daily assessments to find weaknesses in instruction to address (Edutopia, 2015; Bill & Melinda Gates Foundation, 2015).

Understanding How Data is Used

The most common way that administrators use data is by relying on test scores to create improvement goals for their schools (Marsh et al., 2006). This common form of decision-making is exacerbated by the need for administrators to drive their schools to meet state and federal standards. This can actually be a partially detrimental practice, as the integration of data into the improvement of a school is often a shallow practice that stops and ends with meeting state and federal standards (Murray, 2014).

Rather than addressing systemic issues that make effective teaching difficult, school leaders are often satisfied with simply meeting the goals placed upon them by federal and local regulations. The data is often used to monitor specific teachers or students to determine if they require further assistance to meet their goals. One of the ways in which this is most exemplified is by identifying students on the verge of failing proficiency standards set by federal law goals (Murray, 2014). A large number of principals ask teachers to place extra emphasis on boosting the performance of these students who are close to failing their proficiency requirements.

The use of summative data, collected via assessments, typically requires a short time frame with expected turnarounds to occur within a brief time (Datnow, 2017). This is in contrast to a more continuous use of data that informs long-term instructional and organizational improvement. Continuous, long term improvement is more desirable to changes that address issues in the short term and helps students retain more information as well. Schools may be able to make quick changes that improve performance outcomes but fail to address structural issues; however, long term changes may improve outcomes.

Yet another common way in which data is used is to modify curriculum and instructional practices (Marsh et al., 2006). At times, there is a misalignment between the curriculum used and test performance, requiring changes in the curriculum. Administrators rarely use data when deciding which students to promote and those who should be retained (Marsh et al., 2006). Most often, districts and administrators use the data drawn from yearly assessments to adjust curriculum and set instructional guidelines, and not to make decisions involving the future of students or teachers.

Regardless of whether school leaders make changes that are short or long term in nature, they may fail to improve equitable outcomes for all students (Datnow, 2017). The use of standardized tests to inform the majority of a school's changes may inadvertently privilege one student population over another (Datnow, 2017). Long range, continuous improvements may be superior for improving equitable opportunities since these improvements integrate a broader range of data collected from more varied sources.

Data can be used to improve equitable opportunities for students but doing so requires that principals be heavily involved in assessing student progress. This may require sitting with teachers and counselors to address the progress of every student (Datnow, 2017). Given the time intensive nature of such a process, however, this may be problematic, particularly in schools with a high student population, low resources, or both (Datnow, 2017). Principals may instead encourage teachers to look at progress not only from the perspective of academic numerical data, but other data sets, such as behavioral data points, as well.

Improving Decision-Making

Within schools, administrators can improve the integration of data into their decision-making by following certain recommendations (Hamilton et al., 2009). Data can be integrated into part of an ongoing cycle that is used to improve educational instruction. Such cycles can include student assessments, review of curriculum strengths, and the adjustment of that curriculum

(Boudett et al., 2017). The process would then begin once more with future student assessments.

Given the varying levels of the education system at which statistical information has an impact, data driven decisions need to be contextualized by a framework that empowers leaders at each of those levels (Park & Datnow, 2009). While administrators play a crucial role is setting a vision for data driven decision-making in a school, leaders at varying levels of the education system must be empowered to make decisions based on the facts and figures that are available. This grants teachers some authority within their classes; therefore, data driven administrators set agendas while still allowing for some teacher autonomy.

These same leaders set a vision and drive implementation of such decisions within a school, while allocating the resources necessary to create a data driven organization. Principals who employ a data driven decision-making process often empower their teachers to be similarly minded; not only through the delegation of authority, but also setting the vision and allocating resources (Park & Datnow, 2009).

Principals also set a vision for their schools regarding how data is implemented and used to improve the education process (Hamilton et al., 2009). It is vital that principals meet with teachers to reflect on educational practices and make appropriate modifications. School leaders can integrate activities that bring educators and leaders together to identify patterns in data sets and jointly create responses to implement instructional changes (Fenton, n.d.; Stricker, 2017). These meetings can be conducted throughout the year at specific instructional leadership team meetings and faculty meetings (Boudett et al., 2017).

Reviews of data sets can include not only review of academic performance but also behavioral data as well (RTI Network, n.d.). In addition to reviewing data with their teachers, principals might also schedule grade level team meetings as a way to analyze data within a specific group of students. Using the end of year assessments as a base, teachers can provide feedback on what concepts they feel should be more greatly emphasized the following year.

Mentoring to Improve Data Driven Decision-Making

Using statistical data regularly requires that principals foster a data driven culture within their organizations (Hamilton et al., 2009; Boudett et al., 2017). Principals must ensure that new teachers are provided with the coaching necessary to encourage appropriate classroom management and data use. In this capacity, principals are not working with data directly; rather, they are encouraging its integration and use among staff (Marsh, Betrand, & Huguet,

2015). Principals should encourage the development of novice teachers so that they learn how to appropriately extract data from assessments, track student progress, and differentiate their own teaching practices when necessary (Marzano, Warrick, Rains, & DuFour, 2018).

In practice, coaches often play a mediating role in teachers' responses to data (Marsh et al., 2015). Coaches are often critical in helping teachers structure their instructional delivery in a fundamental way. The risk in introducing teachers to data regarding performance is that they may only make superficial changes to their delivery; thus, a coach can help produce a more fundamental shift (Marsh et al., 2015). These in-depth changes occur due to the relationship between a teacher and mentor as well as their deep and thoughtful dialogue exchanges (Marzano et al., 2018). A vertical passing of knowledge from one person to another, as well as a horizontal exchange in which knowledge is co-created, increases the change that occurs (Marsh et al., 2015). All of this occurs within an environment in which school leaders provide a context and basis for change, demonstrating once again how principals can create data driven changes within their organizations.

Principals should use data to guide their decisions and these decisions should encourage their staff to do the same (Hamilton et al., 2009). This is important considering that, even after years of pressure to increase performance and accountability, teachers still fail to properly integrate data-based instructional practices (Wayman & Jimerson, 2014). The decision to implement a form of coaching or mentoring may be critical in helping encourage data driven improvements to classroom instruction (Marsh, McCombs, & Martorell, 2010).

Summative data does not tell a teacher the source of a problem or how to address it; rather, it simply makes clearer that students are either performing up to expectations or missing content that leads to learning gaps. Coaching enables a novice teacher to see a more experienced mentor at work identifying a problem and developing appropriate responses (Marzano et al., 2018). This is illustrative of the problem of looking at data in a vacuum. Providing context for data helps to encourage data driven decision-making. Coaches help to pass on best practices; however, it returns to the principal to create the environment and set up the mentoring relationship to enable data driven decisions in the class (Marsh et al., 2009; Hamilton et al., 2009).

School principals should reflect upon specific questions that encourage data driven decision-making (Marsh & Farrell, 2014). They should assess the data literacy abilities within their organization and ensure that all teachers become data literate. This also requires leaders to assess what resources they have and match those resources to an appropriate instructional method for educators. For some schools, this may mean individual coaching, while other organizations may engage in group instruction (Marsh & Farrell, 2014).

The interventions a leader chooses should reflect the best instructional practices to ensure that teachers come to a robust understanding of data driven decision-making. Finally, principals can dedicate time, create supportive internal policies, and generally exert the leadership required so that their organizations transition to the regular use of data for decision-making at all levels (Marsh & Farrell, 2014). By ensuring that all of these requirements are met, there is a greater likeliness that data will be integrated into decision-making at all levels of an educational organization.

Principals act as a kind of active negotiator between federal guidelines regarding school performance and locally based initiatives (Koyama, 2013). Principals often engage in data driven measures in order to fulfill federal mandates; thus, these principals become active in performing assessments, holding teachers accountable, and taking initiatives that satisfy various federal requirements. Rather than be considered constrained or passive in the face of federal requirements, principals should be considered active agents that work to satisfy the standards placed on their school while also meeting local needs and concerns.

The role of a principal is often one of being actively engaged in making sure a school meets its accountability requirements while also addressing the specific needs of the organizations. By engaging with different forms of data and knowledge, they arrive at decisions that help meet the multiple demands placed upon them both locally and at the federal level (Koyama, 2013).

Data Methods

Part of data driven decision-making includes the process of data collection, storage, and reporting (Halverson, Grigg, Prichett, & Thomas, 2007; Boudett et al., 2017). Halverson et al. (2007), found that schools accessed standardized test scores both through paper reports and online data portals and this data was distributed by both state agencies and test publishing companies. Data was typically composed of both test scores and a range of data points that included demographic data, attendance data, discipline information, expulsion and retention records, and class-based grades (Halverson et al., 2007). In some cases, district offices were central to data collection. At the school level, accurate data collection can be facilitated by the use of computer systems in contrast to physical storage in the form of folders and files (Wayman, 2009).

Collection of data in a digital form also holds the potential for stronger use at the individual school level itself. Through digital storage, student data can be accessed and manipulated in ways that are much more difficult in physical form (Achievement Network, n.d.). These digital records can be manipulated such that comprehensive interpretations about student performance can be derived. Easy availability and manipulation leads to more easily informed instructional modifications. It also makes it easier for principals to hold teachers accountable, since this data can be more easily accessed by school leadership (Wayman, 2009). Reporting to administrators becomes easier for teachers, keeping these administrators better informed of how classes are performing.

The data storage methods examined by Halverson et al. (2007) included using low tech methods such as filing cabinets as well as high tech, computer-based storage and data warehouses. In some cases, schools relied on district support to develop data warehousing technology that could be used for storage purposes, and these systems were often distinct and independent from district data storage systems (Halverson et al., 2007).

Regardless of the storage methods used, all schools are required to have a system for data reporting (Halverson et al., 2007). Such reporting included data exchanged between schools and district data as well as information exchanged professionally between teachers and school administrators. As such, the data pipeline included both internal school information exchanges and information exchanges with district level data centers, which allowed for the collection of data from multiple sources (Halverson et al., 2007).

The Eight Step Data Wise Improvement Process

The eight steps of the Data Wise Improvement Process provide a framework for educators that helps to focus meetings, produces challenging and thought-provoking questions, allows for deep discussions, and sets the stage for actionable strategies for each student based on data that is irrefutable (Boudett et al., 2017). While it is not mandatory to follow the Data Wise cycle, this type of data-driven decision-making tool provides an easy to follow action plan.

The eight steps help principals guide teachers to design questions as they go through the inquiry process to deepen their work through metacognition (Boudett et al., 2017). Equally important, teachers can use this cycle without the principal to work through data. Each phase has specific action steps that teachers can think deeply about; thus, creating an action plan based on student data and teaching practices (Boudett et al., 2017).

- Step 1: Organize for collaborative work that focuses on designing teams and defining the norms that the group will follow.
- Step 2: Build assessment literacy that is centered on the team understanding common terms and becomes knowledgeable of the data that will be used in the inquiry phase.
- Step 3: Create data overview and the questions that will be used to understand what the data represents in terms of student learning.
- Step 4: Dig deeper into student data and identify student-learning problems.
- Step 5: Examine the instruction utilized and define problems of practice.
- Step 6: Lengthy discussion then ensues on methods to use to develop a plan or instructional strategies.
- Step 7: Design a plan to assess student progress in terms of short, medium and long-term goals while stage eight acts on the plan and reassesses.
- Step 8: Document improvements in the teaching and learning process, adjust teaching practice, and begin the cycle again.

Data Wise's success lies in that it is cyclical in nature, offers a clear and easy to follow step-by-step format, and offers principals and educators a real-time snapshot of student achievement so that educators can create lesson plans and student experiences that are meaningful (Boudett et al., 2017).

Principals as Data Driven Decision-Makers

Whether principals decide to rely on data to inform their decisions is reliant on their attitudes toward the value of data itself (Buske & Zlatkin-Troitschanskaia, 2018). Principals, like all others, bring a certain set of values and beliefs to their roles. Some are more skeptical than others regarding how data can be used to improve academic performance. A greater amount of confidence in the ability of data to transform a school's performance may make it more likely that principals will make data-informed decisions (Buske & Zlatkin-Troitschanskaia, 2018).

When principals do use data, how it is used varies based on organization related factors (Luo, 2008). How accessible data is and whether data collection is mandated at the district level affect how principals use the data. Even when they do use it, the data tends to inform changes in altering instructional practices or organization related factors (Murray, 2014). Rarely is data used to create changes in leadership, such as changes in school vision or the creation of collaborative partnerships (Luo, 2008). Such findings reflect how even robust data is limited in its applicability by principals themselves.

Some school leaders simply are unfamiliar with the appropriate use of data (Mense & Crain-Dorough, 2018). A school may have multiple avenues by which data is collected and yet still lack an ability to take that data and make it actionable. Quantitative data, including attendance, grade performance, and behavior are regularly collected, while qualitative data collected by school personnel is often easily available as well; however, school leaders often fail to create a culture necessary for integrating data (Bowers, Shoho, & Barnett, 2014).

Schoolwide impact is driven by the principal through instructional practices. Without leadership, it cannot be assumed that teachers will simply integrate data into their practices, since many educators are either resistant or apprehensive to informing their practices in this manner (Mense & Crain-Dorough, 2018). Leaders and teachers often continue to base their practices on perceptions and anecdotes rather than the data available to them. When school leaders do integrate data, they sometimes do so in such a way that is distanced from best practices (Mense & Crain-Dorough, 2018). This creates a phenomenon in which data is used so poorly that there is a gap between what research implies the difference between what a school can accomplish and where they land at the end of the year.

A full 69% of principals studied reported that their leadership preparation programs were inadequate with regard to training in how to lead an educational organization (Hale & Moorman, 2003). Most concerning, principals reported that their programs focused more on leadership theory rather than on practical ways of addressing school-based issues. These problems are exacerbated by the lack of partnerships with schools allowing for direct experience prior to becoming a school administrator.

Principals must be well-acquainted with using data in a way that leads to improved schoolwide outcomes (Bill & Melinda Gates Foundation, 2015; Bowers et al., 2014). School leaders must be able to strengthen the learning process using data driven decisions, as such, changes in leadership programs are necessary as a means to ensure that well qualified administrators are able to meet the modern challenges of leading schools.

Final Thoughts

Part of becoming prepared for 21st century school leadership includes becoming data literate and understanding the effective integration of data to inform decisions (Bowers et al., 2014). For school leaders, this can include taking multiple steps in their use of data to include which data sources they use, and how they use it (Marsh et al., 2015).

It is vital that school leaders be familiar with statistical concepts and measurements. At least some familiarity with statistical concepts helps leaders to better understand the data they are presented with. Finally, leaders should be able to draw conclusions from data and statistical analysis (Earl & Katz, 2002). These suppositions can then be integrated into the data decision making process when addressing issues within a school.

Points to Remember

- *At its heart, data driven decision making is the ability of school leaders and educators to use the results from student assessments to improve teaching and learning.*
- *When properly implemented, making data-informed decisions provides a platform for the improved achievement for all students as expected by state and federal mandates.*
- *Feedback systems rely on a cyclical process that includes teaching, assessment, reflection, and altering teaching.*
- *Summative high-stakes testing rarely influences actual teaching due to the spring test season and delayed results; thus, formative assessments are necessary to influence adjustments to teaching that have school-wide implications.*
- *Based on school-wide goals, Instructional leadership teams can determine the data criteria, examine the assessment results, and influence educator teaching methods.*

Chapter 6

Earning an 'A' in Instructional Leadership: Promoting Continuous Improvement Through Deliberate Practices

Leadership has been attributed as being among the most important factors in determining the academic outcomes of schools (Harris et al., 2013). The quality of leadership is important since principals have to manage so many systems, from teacher instructional methods to budgets. The quality of leadership has also become increasingly important as the competition between schools to raise standards and academic outcomes has risen over the last few years.

What is Instructional Leadership

Instructional leadership is characterized by school administrators who create a culture that prioritizes instruction and assessment in a cyclical manner (Baeder, 2018). These leaders place students at the center of the instructional process, while also facilitating the professional development of educators. School leaders who employ an instructional leadership style are often effective at setting a school's mission, managing a school's curriculum, monitoring and improving teacher instruction, creating a positive learning environment, and generally providing oversight of all points of instruction (Baeder, 2018; Glickman, Gordon, & Ross-Gordon, 2018; Loveless, 2016).

Through the process of leading, principals empower others to be influential members of the educational team. Instructional leaders facilitate the development of others. Teachers then become their own circle of support in which they help to improve the instructional skills of one another (Glickman et al., 2018). Despite several authors who have deliberately defined and explained instructional leadership, specific practices employed by leaders differ (Baeder, 2018; Glickman et al., 2018; Loveless, 2016).

Traditionally, instructional leadership has been centered on principals (Neumerski, 2012). Other areas of research have involved instructional leadership as employed by teachers and coaches; however, a comprehensive understanding of the topic continues to lag. Consequently, there have been recommendations that more comprehensive research be conducted into how instructional leadership is demonstrated in the education system (Neumerski, 2012).

One way that instructional leadership is often conceptualized includes leaders who bring both expertise and charisma to their roles (Burgess & Houf, 2017; Hallinger, 2010). These leaders are active in the coordination of curriculum and work directly with teachers to improve performance (Glickman et al., 2018). They typically remain goal oriented and focus changes on creating specific improvements to academic outcomes. Very often, principals are responsible for the creation of a school's culture (Baeder, 2018; Hallinger, 2010). This includes setting high expectations for both students and teachers, suggesting that instructional leaders rely on their experience and charisma to produce a culture shift in the organizations they become a part of.

Fairly consistently, instructional leaders are characterized as individuals who are highly engaged with staff to meet measurable goals (Hallinger, 2010). They supervise and evaluate instruction, coordinate curriculum, and monitor student progress. These leaders also promote the professional development of their staff, are typically highly visible, provide incentives for teachers, and provide the appropriate instructional time for teachers (Glickman et al., 2018; Burgess & Houf, 2017).

Instructional leadership has also been differentiated between traditional concepts that revolve around improving individual staff performance versus organization level revisions that bring about structural change (Horng & Loeb, 2010). Traditional concepts regarding instructional leadership ideas focused on actions such as classroom observations and feedback. Under the more traditional conceptualization of instructional leadership, principals focused primarily on revising curriculum and improving teacher instruction (Horng & Loeb, 2010).

These hands-on leaders are directly engaged with teachers and often act as mentors (Horng & Loeb, 2010). While this may work in some cases, principals charged with leading larger schools may simply lack the resources and time necessary for being engaged in all aspects of the school - given the many classes within their organization. Principals in larger schools offering broader coursework, for example, would be particularly challenged to help revise curriculum in areas where personal content knowledge was lacking.

Principals may be able to more broadly impact academic outcomes by improving their hiring methods, more expertly aligning teachers to specific classes, improving retention methods, and creating opportunities for teacher improvement (Marzano et al., 2018; Horng & Loeb, 2010). This newer conceptualization of instructional leadership does not exclude practices that characterized the older model, rather, the new model of instructional leadership provides principals with additional options that may have more wide-ranging impact, options that are necessary particularly when a school is of great size (Marzano et al., 2018; Horng & Loeb, 2010). Instructional leadership should be conceptualized as an organization-wide process rather than classroom level intervention method in many cases (Glickman et al., 2018).

Instructional leadership includes both direct and indirect interventions (Bendikson, Robinson, & Hattie, 2012). Under this conceptualization, direct instructional leadership has to do with creating interventions that directly influence teachers' teaching practices. Indirect instructional leadership, on the other hand, has to do with creating the conditions necessary for good instruction. Both types of instructional leadership must be practiced simultaneously in order to help improve school performance (Bendikson et al., 2012).

Returning to the issue of organization level changes, Halverson and Clifford (2013) conducted a study on distributed instructional leadership and suggested that such a model could be effective in producing positive changes within a school. Distributed instructional leadership requires that administrators determine how the current interaction between tools, tasks, and routines creates and perpetuates an existing system of learning (Halverson & Clifford, 2013).

Only by first evaluating those tools, tasks, and routines will leaders begin to establish new routines that create organization-wide change by altering the learning culture (Halverson & Clifford, 2013). Consequently, using distributed leadership as a model, administrators must assess all factors in order to begin implementing meaningful reform. The sum result of years of research is that there are multiple conceptualizations of what constitutes instructional leadership (Bodnarchuk, 2016). The one consistent emerging result from research, however, is that instructional leadership is best embodied in the role of the principal (Bodnarchuck, 2016; Marzano et al., 2018).

The majority of existing literature revolves around how principals impact the schools in which they work by demonstrating the characteristics associated with instructional leadership (Bodnarchuk, 2016; Glickman et al., 2018; Baeder, 2018; Marzano et al., 2018). Several common characteristics have been adopted by various researchers to guide studies to include creating clear goals, promoting professional development, and overseeing curriculum; yet the definition for instructional leadership continues to take on slightly different meanings (Bodnarchuk, 2016; Glickman et al., 2018; Baeder, 2018; Marzano et al., 2018).

Implementation of Instructional Leadership

Principals can employ the same methods and experience varied effects, with the differences in outcomes often illustrating the level of instructional leader effectiveness (Glickman et al., 2018; Marzano et al., 2018). In a Wallace Foundation study (2013), for example, principals were rated either high or low as instructional leaders; yet they all made frequent classroom visits within their schools and were considered visible within their communities.

The difference lies in the purpose behind why each principal visited these classrooms. Principals who scored highly made frequent classroom visits for brief periods of time (The Wallace Foundation, 2013; Glickman et al., 2018). These were spontaneous visits that were used to make formative observations and provide immediate classroom feedback. These highly scoring principals aimed at improving the performance of teachers and felt that teachers of all experience levels still have room to grow (The Wallace Foundation, 2013). In contrast, low performing principals often gave advanced warning to their teachers, did not use their visits for instructional purposes, and provided little in the way of feedback to their staff (Glickman et al., 2018).

The ongoing effort to distribute leadership among staff and provide data for teacher improvement may be tied to the increased self-efficacy that teachers feel (Calik, Sezgin, Ferudun, Kavgaci, & Killinc, 2012). A study of 328 classrooms and teachers in various primary schools revealed that instructional leadership positively impacted feelings of collective self-efficacy (Calik et al., 2012).

Consequently, as a collective, teachers believed in their ability to provide instruction (Calik et al., 2012). These results again revealed how instructional leaders influence their staff. Consistent with the early research by Fowler and Walter (2003), Calik et al. (2012) demonstrated that instructional leaders helped to empower their teaching staff. Teachers then operate with greater confidence apart from needing constant encouragement from leadership. These findings underscore that instructional leadership plays a critical role in creating a confident staff.

Opportunities for Collaboration

Instructional leaders also provided chances for teachers to collaborate (Lunenburg, 2010; Baeder, 2018; Glickman et al., 2018). Principals who encourage an environment in which students are the focus, generally help align teacher expectations with instructional goals. With goals aligned, principals facilitate increased engagement between teachers so that the staff becomes collectively engaged in achieving the newly aligned goals (Baeder, 2018; Marzano et al., 2018).

This collective engagement is an important aspect of effective instruction (Lunenburg, 2010). When there is an appropriate environment and support, teachers are more likely to pursue the organization's goals. The principal, therefore, plays a critical role in encouraging teachers to work together toward schoolwide goals. Sustained engagement and interaction helps to make teachers more willing to adapt to new research-based information that can improve instructional delivery (Glickman et al., 2018).

Among the most common forms of collaborative engagement is the use of teacher teams (Lunenburg, 2010). These teams identify what students should know, design curriculum and instructional strategies, create a process for evaluating those strategies, and both analyze results and revise strategies where necessary (Baeder, 2018). Teacher teams, therefore, are responsible for constantly creating and revising ideas that are used in an individual teacher's classroom.

Influencing Instruction through Leadership

At least one study indicated that instructional leadership manifested in one of three ways (Rigby, 2013). This study was designed to examine how principals conceptualized instructional leadership and how their practices manifested in the organizations in which they practiced (Rigby, 2013). Given the impact that school leaders have on an instructional institution and student academic outcomes, those who conceptualized their leadership style were given higher ratings (Rigby, 2013).

Generally, instructional leadership was flexibly conceived and without the consistent practices that characterized such a style (Rigby, 2013). Instructional leadership was a broad conception without specific directions for how to implement it. Some principals engaged in a specific form deemed entrepreneurial instructional leadership (Rigby, 2013). Leaders in this classification were characterized by innovative behaviors and practices that mirrored those in the private sector (Rigby, 2013).

Entrepreneurial principals were heavily reliant on data to take actions that improved outcomes (Rigby, 2013). A second strain of instructional leadership was also found. This social justice form of instructional leadership was oriented around improving the experiences of students at the margins (Rigby, 2013). Overlooked and marginalized groups were championed by these leaders to help reduce inequities between students.

The results of this study make clear that instructional leaders can engage in widely varying practices that seek to improve school conditions in numerous ways (Glickman et al., 2018; Rigby, 2013). Some look at data to improve academic outcomes while others hope to improve school culture and benefit marginalized groups. Principals would be wise to learn to practice in both areas out of a hope of improving outcomes for students in multiple ways (Glickman et al., 2018).

Curriculum Articulation, Cross-Program Activities, and Strategic Staffing

Another examination of instructional leadership practices indicated that there were three forms of broad instructional leadership practiced (Lee, Hallinger, & Walker, 2012). These practices included curriculum articulation, cross-program activities, and strategic staffing. The practice of curriculum articulation included finding connections between school programs. This occurred after leaders identified missing links in curriculum between different programs (Lee et al., 2012).

Curriculum articulation was used to ensure that students acquired the necessary skills they would use as they progressed in their education (Lee et al., 2012). Curriculum development teams, for instance, were assembled to examine curriculum used throughout a school to identify gaps in learning. To help teachers learn more about other programs within the school, cross-program activities were also implemented (Lee et al., 2012).

These activities encouraged educators to communicate with one another in staff meetings and schoolwide workshops (Lee et al., 2012). Teachers collaborated with one another in the form of cross-program professional development. In some cases, teachers were given opportunities to teach in more than one program or coordinate different programs. This allowed for further integration of different programs and greater familiarity between teachers with programs they typically did not lead. This also contributed to the schoolwide sense of community and perspective of distributed leadership (Lee et al., 2012).

Finally, in these schools, principals attempted to strategically hire (Lee et al., 2012). This included intentionally bringing educators onboard with pertinent experience so that they could be more quickly aligned with the school's philosophies and goals (Lee et al., 2012). In other words, principals engaged in hiring practices that allowed for teachers to be integrated into their programs far more quickly than if these teachers lacked the appropriate experience.

District Support for Leaders

With all that principals can do and the ways that they can act as instructional leaders, it is vital that school leaders be supported by their districts (Louis & Robinson, 2012). These administrators do not exhibit leadership in a vacuum; rather, their actions are contextualized by responsibilities to their staff as well as their need to meet external accountability mandates (Louis & Robinson, 2012).

Principals are continuously called upon to help meet external district goals (Louis & Robinson, 2012). To ensure that leaders are most effective in their actions, principals values should be in alignment with the policies established at the district level. External accountability policies have a positive impact on the leadership practices of principals when they align with a school leader's own values (Louis & Robinson, 2012).

When districts demonstrate that they are supportive of a principal's initiatives, this also has a positive impact on leadership practice (Marzano & Waters, 2009). Under these circumstances, school leaders internalize the external policies placed upon them and find ways to address the needs within their schools to meet those accountability standards. Internalization helps engage school leaders, who can then align their schools' specific priorities with the mandates (Louis & Robinson, 2012). When there is a lack of alignment, principals tend to hold more negative views, which negatively impacts their performance (Louis & Robinson, 2012). To create engaged leaders and optimal outcomes, accountability mandates should align with a principal's values (Marzano & Waters, 2009).

Meaningful Staff Conversations

Yet another issue that arises when discussing the effectiveness of principals is the inability to have conversations with staff regarding performance issues (Le Fevre & Robinson, 2014). The researchers noted that it wasn't uncommon for principals to struggle with effective communication with their staff regarding existing issues and they tended to be tolerant and protective of their teachers (Le Fevre & Robinson, 2014). They had a tendency to avoid addressing confrontational issues rather than deal with them in an effective way. The researchers concluded that in many circumstances, principals only demonstrated, at most, a moderate ability to have difficult conversations regarding performance with teachers (Le Fevre & Robinson, 2014).

While a principal could often elaborate on their own position, they were rarely skilled in exploring the views of their teachers (Le Fevre & Robinson, 2014). The implication of such findings was that leaders needed to increase in their interpersonal skills. In order to improve the performance of their staff, principals needed to be more engaged and learn how to have effective, though respectful, discussions regarding instructional qualities (Boston, Henrick, Gibbons, Berebitsky, & Colby, 2017). These study results demonstrated, yet again, the many ways in which principals could be instructed to become more effective instructional leaders.

Special Education Considerations

Another facet of instructional leadership implementation includes addressing the needs of special education students (Zaretsky, Moreau, & Faircloth, 2008). An ongoing need is to encourage equitable opportunities for all students. Consequently, assessment of instructional leaders has included assessing the outcomes within special education programs (Glickman et al., 2018). The needs of special education students require specific knowledge and skills that principals sometimes lack, owing to a lack of specialized training.

In order to fulfill the goal of being leaders who can improve outcomes for all students, principals noted their desire for increased preparation in special education during their leadership programs as such knowledge would help to improve outcomes for special education students (Zaretsky et al., 2008). Specific training could bolster the already existing abilities of leaders to draw upon research-based practices; thus, improving instructional methods in the classroom (Zaretsky et al., 2008). The information gleaned from the study was a reminder that to truly encourage instructional leadership, principals themselves had to be fully prepared to encourage improved outcomes for all students, including those participating in special education programs.

Connecting Leadership Practices to Academic Performance

Another difficulty encountered in the study of instructional leadership is the lack of evidence connecting instructional leadership, as broadly defined, with improvements in school performance (Grissom et al., 2013). In a unique study of principals, researchers performed in-person observations throughout a whole day, watching the behaviors of 100 urban principals over the course of 3 academic years (Grissom et al., 2013). The researchers found no evidence that, generally speaking, the practices used by principals helped to improve academic performance (Grissom et al., 2013).

Despite finding little evidence that school performance increased due to the general implementation of instructional leadership, there were specific instructional behaviors that were connected to improved student achievement to include teacher coaching, ongoing evaluations of performance, and regular development of a school's education program (Grissom et al., 2013).

Effective practices, therefore, revolve around improving curriculum and instructional delivery; yet other practices had no impact (Grissom et al., 2013). Informal walkthroughs of classrooms negatively predicted student growth. The researchers hypothesized that this was due to the fact that principals did not use the walkthroughs as a means of improving their schools' operations (Grissom et al., 2013). The study revealed that simply being an involved principal was not, of itself, sufficient for improving school performance; rather, principals had to integrate what they learned into a cycle of improving instructional delivery by providing teachers with opportunities to improve their instructional methods (Grissom et al., 2013).

Initial Implementation of Instructional Leadership

Large scale school reform assessments were observed in one instance to help principals begin a transition to instructional leadership (Prytula, Noonan, & Hellsten, 2013). These assessments were valued by school leaders and initiated new practices that aligned with instructional leadership concepts. The relevance of assessment to curricular content was specifically found to be important in helping initiate changes. This led to new practices on the part of principals.

School leaders were not always aware that their changes were consistent with instructional leadership; rather, they were drawing on the data to initiate changes that aligned with instructional leadership practices out of their own instincts (Prytula et al., 2013). Principals attempted to empower their teachers and use assessments to improve instructional practices. The focus of these changes was on improving learning and academic outcomes; yet the changes were inconsistent from one school to another, and the researchers noted that school leaders often lacked the knowledge and skills required to make fully informed shifts in practice (Prytula et al., 2013).

In other cases, principals simply did not integrate the data from assessments (Prytula et al., 2013). It appeared that in some cases, these leaders did not see the relevance between the results of these assessments and the curriculum being used in the school. Prytula et al. (2013) hypothesized that the greater the connection and relevance between curriculum and assessments, the more likely that principals would be receptive to using those assessments to inform teaching practices within their schools. To help ensure that appropriate changes were made by school leaders, there must be appropriate support to help introduce the skills and knowledge necessary to make effective change in the classrooms.

Obstacles that Prevent Implementation of Instructional Leadership Practices

In some cases, a sheer lack of experience makes it difficult to implement new leadership practices, while some principals may not be effective in the implementation of instructional changes among teaching staff (Sofo, Fitzgerald, & Jawas, 2012) These school leaders also lack resources and support from central authorities in many cases, illustrating how obstacles to leadership reform can sometimes be the product of failure to support school leaders.

School leaders are also not always empowered by central authorities to introduce new changes that can benefit schools.

It may not even be possible to make effective changes when the national curriculum changes rapidly, again highlighting the problems created outside of the local school level (Sofo et al., 2012). The lack of effectiveness at the national level impacts what principals can do, making it impossible to institute cultural changes within their schools. What emerges are schools that constantly have to deal with curriculum changes. These schools also lack empowered leaders who can implement leadership changes and institute a new school culture (Sofo et al., 2012).

Attempts to implement instructional leadership have met with mixed results (Hallinger & Lee, 2013). The reform of leadership practices in Thailand, for example, has been relatively unsuccessful due to confusion in what actually constitutes instructional leadership (Hallinger & Lee, 2013). When countries make a shift toward instructional leadership, it involves a cultural change that schools may not be prepared to accomplish. Employing new techniques and methods may be difficult in countries that have long practiced traditional leadership methods.

Since the reforms introduced by Thailand's National Education Act of 1999, principals have continued to use traditional approaches and continue to be oriented toward practicing leadership styles that have long been in use (Hallinger & Lee, 2013). These conditions have made a shift to instructional leadership difficult, and a relatively small number of Thai principals employ methods associated with instructional leadership approaches.

Indonesia encountered similar cultural difficulties in transitioning toward an instructional leadership model (Sofo et al., 2012). Attempts to introduce reforms in the country have been introduced on the national level; however, the actual leadership practices in place at the school level have not been changed in many cases. Despite the importance of school leadership in improving student academic outcomes, many obstacles prevent effective implementation of instructional leadership.

Similarly, attempts to implement instructional leadership in Turkish primary schools also failed (Gumus & Akcaoglu, 2013). Research into the implementation of new leadership styles in Turkey revealed that principals did not implement changes on a regular basis that were consistent with instructional leadership, rather, they only occasionally used these new strategies (Gumus & Akcaoglu, 2013). Such findings were indicative of the difficulty in implementing instructional leadership for the first time as even when principals adopted such measures, they might not apply them with the consistency necessary to effect significant changes (Gumus & Akcaoglu, 2013).

Final Thoughts

Instructional leaders are able to set the stage for success through specific and pre-determined actions that guide educators in a process that is cyclical in nature. Using instruction and assessment, leaders and educators examine data to determine how to improve processes associated with positive outcomes. Professional development activities and administrator feedback ensure educators use every teaching strategy possible to reach all students regardless of ability. Although instructional leadership may not always be clearly defined, current studies are providing a path forward that includes strategies and practices that administrators can use to help educators improve their teaching practice, in turn supporting students in their quest for academic success.

Points to Remember

- *Instructional leadership prioritizes instruction and assessment in a cyclical manner to improve student outcomes.*

- *Administrators who value instructional leadership go to great lengths to place students at the center of the instructional process.*

- *Principals who employ instructional leadership are adept at setting a school mission and vision, creating a positive culture, and determining the curriculum needs of all students.*

- *Instructional leaders are hands-on administrators and often engage with staff members as mentors to ensure proper coaching takes place.*

- *Professional development for staff is an essential piece of the instructional process. It must be continuous and focused, and it must allow for periods of educator practice.*

Chapter 7

Valuing Equity, Equality, and Inclusive Practices: Fostering Achievement in Diverse Populations

In order to address equity in learning, there exists a host of questions that must be considered and, in some way, answered. Principals must consider how equity in learning fosters a positive school culture; one that students, faculty, and families can learn and grow in. The very role of the principal in creating a positive school culture might be questioned as well as the responsibility of the community in ensuring equitable practices are evident in school culture and learning. The principal must safeguard that the teaching population mirrors its students. Finally, district equity policies must be implemented in both urban and rural areas.

Most districts have an equity policy that delineates how equity in learning will be implemented; yet over time, the meaning of the policy has not kept pace with an ever-evolving world of equity. As the population of each district changes, it is not easy to alter the school culture fast enough to keep pace with the factors that impact education institutions.

Defining Equity

The make-up of an American classroom has changed significantly since the Brown decision in 1954. At that time, African Americans embraced 11 percent of the student population while white students made up 85% of the classes (Center for Public Education (CPE), 2016). Since that time, a population change of approximately 20 % has occurred with the white population now at 63%, while the other 37% consists of people of color (Frey, 2016). In many schools, particularly in urban areas, people of color and the Hispanic population represent the majority of students (National Center for Education Statistics, 2015).

The Center for Public Education (2016) defines equality as a time when "children are all treated the same and have access to similar resources [whereas,] equity is achieved when all students receive the resources they need" (p. 1) to be successful in school. An easy way to remember the difference is that equality is the same treatment and similar resources; whereas, equity is treatment tailored to the needs of the student and full access to resources.

As the first federal regulation of Brown v. the Board of Education in 1954 sought to remedy issues of segregation, it actually created more issues than first thought. Simmons (2014) cites "inequitable distribution of resources for African American students, seriously hampering and undermining their academic achievement" (n.p.). In 1983, A Nation at Risk changed the focus from educational and social needs to attaining economic competitiveness on the backs of students (Simmons, 2014). The No Child Left Behind Act in 2001granted states permission to develop their own legislation and educational strategies, and, as such, the inequities and disparities of education grew as did the achievement gap (Simmons, 2014).

The continuation of using these poorly founded legislations, deficit thinking, and non-growth mindsets, as opposed to finding and building on student strengths, would certainly prolong disparities and inequities in education based on subgroups and their specific characteristics (NCES, 2015). Newer legislation such as the Elementary and Secondary Education Act (ESSA) is focused on the socio-cultural context of the current student population by concentrating on the development of different types of learning that take into consideration the positive attributes of these students and their families (Simmons, 2014). This type of thinking will lead to renewed teaching and learning methods that will catapult students towards college and career readiness.

Other demographic factors that cause educators to think about equity in their daily practices include children living in poverty, English language learners, those who come to school with little foundation knowledge, and those with large academic gaps (CPE, 2016). The Center for Social Inclusion (2017) defines racial equity as achieving it "when race no longer determines one's socioeconomic outcomes" (n.p.). This means that everyone should have what he or she requires to live and be successful, that isn't dependent on where one lives or their zip code. As educators, we can apply equity through every usable lens and to everything we do, especially those impacted by structural inequity (Center for Social Inclusion, 2017).

Understanding Structural Inequality

Structural inequalities are biases that are grown over time within organizations, schools, and cultures that provide advantages for some while others do not benefit from the same treatment, experiences, access to services, housing, medical care and education or academic services (DeMatthews & Mawhinney,

2014). These inequalities also manifest themselves in fund distribution, highly qualified teachers, and technology. Over time these inequalities manifest themselves deeper and deeper into a group or institution until they become part of the fabric of an entity (Bogotch, Schoorman, Reyes-Guerra, 2017).

Educational budgets are one of the first inequities, so much so that the disparity between communities within the same state for the cost per pupil may be tremendous (DeMatthews & Mawhinney, 2014). Communities often compete for their fair share of a state budget while local communities may contribute more than others. Wealthy counterparts usually in suburban areas outdo their neighboring urban communities (Maciag, 2016). Within small geographical areas discrepancies within funding affect poorly on some communities while other do well (Maciag, 2016).

Urban communities typically have high proportions of second language learners and students who qualify for free and reduced meals, which reveal high levels of poverty and a low tax basis (CPE, 2016). Title 1 was built on the assumption that educating students who live in poverty are 40 percent more expensive than those without such a designation (Bogotch et al., 2017). A low tax base often inhibits the community's ability to have a higher cost per student expenditure (Bogotch et al., 2017). Districts with students requiring special education services are obliged to meet strict IDEA guidelines that raise educational costs.

Educational expenditures are only part of the equity equation. Students who require more skill development necessitate the use of high-level curriculums and interventions that mediate their learning deficits (Alexander & Jang, 2017). These curricula are essential and when possible, should be offered early in a child's education, perhaps in pre-school. Children who are able to begin kindergarten with skills and content knowledge that are on a level with peers maintain their skills and are able to progress through school showing positive growth areas (Young, Jean, & Mead, 2019).

Other areas of the equity equation are well-trained teachers and instructional staff that are knowledgeable about researched-based interventions and other methodologies that are used to equalize student learning (CPE, 2016). Accommodations are made so that each student has what he or she needs to be successful; this is not optional, rather it is obligatory for all educators (Adelman & Taylor, 2018). Strategies that include utilizing all of the sensory components and/or tiered interventions are required for all students in need (Young, Jean, & Mead, 2019).

System changes need to be maintained or changed to build success. When ESSA was enacted, the different components of the original NCLB around testing were preserved (Egalite, Fusarelli, & Fusarelli, 2017). The testing measures required in grades 3 through 8 and during high school continue to look at the progress of the subgroupings; however, states are now responsible for corrective actions (Egalite et al., 2017). These system changes are being implemented differently from area to area. The changes in oversight by the federal government and turning over more accountability to states has created different versions of culpability that may impact cross-state professional development. The decentralization of educational policy may become problematic to states, local education agencies and schools.

Supporting Inclusive Practices for Diverse Populations

A challenge that all school systems face is ensuring that inclusive practices are apparent in teaching pedagogy, implementation of curriculum, and transparent within and between educators, principals, and families (McLeskey & Waldron, 2015). The new reality of changing student demographics increases the need for principals to examine how they develop a culture where all students are welcomed, supported for their individual needs, feel accepted, valued and safe (Young, Jean, & Mead, 2019). As such, it is imperative that schools employ pedagogies that recognize the social identity of their students, families, and teaching staff.

Defining Inclusive Practice

Inclusive practice is a philosophy of inclusion that changes teachers and principal thinking and actions to include children from other countries, those with disabilities, families who have other values and beliefs based on their culture, and those who have varied backgrounds, learning styles and abilities (D'Auria, 2015). Other skills that leaders need to think about include distinguishing between the 'what' and 'how' of circumstances that often goes beyond daily principal duties (D'Auria, 2015). Learning skills that help others achieve are often not part of a leadership skill set; rather, they must be learned and modeled for educators (D'Auria, 2015). Reaching out to more veteran or experienced educational leaders often can support the ever-growing skill sets of principals.

Supporting Inclusive Practices

When teachers are not feeling prepared to deal with an inclusive teaching practice, the role of the principal increases to provide more support and a commitment to core values. Teacher preparation programs are limited in their scope to include instruction that covers all the nuances of culture and inclusion; thus, it becomes the role of the principal to fill in these voids. Discussions that begin with the core values of staff and leadership reinforces the foundation that inclusive practices are built upon. Principals, with effective leadership skills, who use varied strategies to implement new initiatives, will see increased school culture that supports inclusion (Hollingworth et al., 2015).

Principals who use an equity lens to support teachers in using inclusionary practices that are best for all children reveal that their schools are better prepared to work with children from all backgrounds and all abilities (Veeriah et al., 2017). Being able to confront these challenges with professionalism and knowledge of research will enable teachers to be effective in implementing research-based practices and cultural-based curricula (Williams, Brien, & LeBlanc, 2012).

Gender Identity and Sexual Orientation

Federal law Title IX protects all students from sexual discrimination in school and ensures that students are "respected and can learn in an accepting environment" (U.S. Department of Education, n.d.b, n.p.). Likewise, the Family Educational Rights and Privacy Act (FERPA) protects students' privacy and educational records (U.S. Department of Education, n.d.c). These federal laws set the ground rules and the bare minimum acceptable for states to build on.

As an example of one state's efforts to protect students, the Massachusetts Department of Elementary and Secondary Education (n.d.) released a non-discrimination policy that acted on the belief that echoed the intent of the federal law. This document covers the definitions related to gender identity, the law, understanding gender identity and gender transition, names and pronouns, and issues related to FERPA (Massachusetts Department of Elementary and Secondary Education, n.d.). Other topics included in the document include locker room/restroom facilities, physical education and intramural sports, home-school-community communications, and education and training for staff (Massachusetts Department of Elementary and Secondary Education, n.d.).

To ensure a common understanding of gender identity and sexual orientation as it relates to school-aged children, it is necessary to define common terms used to describe gender differences:

- "*Gender expression:* the manner in which a person represents or expresses gender to others, often through behavior, clothing, hairstyles, activities, voice, or mannerisms" (Massachusetts Department of Elementary and Secondary Education, n.d.)
- "*Gender identity:* a person's gender-related identity, appearance or behavior, whether or not that gender-related identity, appearance or behavior is different from that traditionally associated with the per-

son's physiology or assigned sex at birth" (U.S. Department of Education, n.d.b, n.p.).

- *"Gender nonconforming:* a term used to describe people whose gender expression differs from stereotypical expectations" (Massachusetts Department of Elementary and Secondary Education, n.d.).

- *"Transgender:* an umbrella term used to describe a person whose gender identity or gender expression is different from that traditionally associated with the assigned sex at birth" (Massachusetts Department of Elementary and Secondary Education, n.d.).

The Massachusetts document, similar to other states, is detailed and seeks to ensure the well-being of students through a supportive school culture (Massachusetts Department of Elementary and Secondary Education, n.d.). While this topic can be confusing, and somewhat gray at times, the most important thing to remember is that a student who identifies as one sex or the other for most of the time, should be treated as that gender (Massachusetts Department of Elementary and Secondary Education, n.d.).

In terms of harassment of sexual minority and gender diverse youth, the statistics are sobering. According to a 2012 survey, 71% of these students heard negative comments made by peers, while 57% heard staff make negative comments (Kosciw, Greytak, Bartkiewicz, Boesen, & Palmer, 2012). The statistics for bullying behavior towards sexual minority and gender diverse students are no better with 82% having been verbally harassed, while 38% had been physically harassed (Kosciw et al., 2012). This presents quite a problem for school leaders who aim to provide a safe haven for all students, and especially for gender diverse and sexual minority students.

A report published by the American Psychological Association in 2015 offers key recommendations for school administrators to support students who fall under the Title IX umbrella.

- Inclusive environment: Create a climate where bullying and discrimination is not tolerated; rather, diversity is seen as a positive and the school culture is accepting of all gender expressions.

- Inform and educate: Principals and staff are responsible for understanding the issues surrounding gender diversity and sexual orientation. Resources such as the counselor and other support staff, as well as professional development opportunities must be available.

- Home-school connections: Principals should work closely with families to find supports that match the needs of the student. Regular and open communication is essential as is connecting the student and family to the school counselor or psychologist who can better guide, listen, and connect the family to services as needed.

- Privacy vs need to know: Develop a plan to share personal information with those who need to know underscoring the importance of FERPA and confidentiality.

- Basic rights: School leaders are responsible for ensuring that gender neutral bathrooms and locker rooms are available for students who choose to use them, while students should feel safe in choosing sports and physical education activities that match their chosen gender or sexual orientation. Equally important, names and pronouns that properly correspond to students' gender expression should be valued and consistently used by staff and other students.

Immigrants and Children of Immigrants

2015 marked the year that there were fewer than 50 percent white students in the K12 public schools of the United States and by 2023 this number has the potential to go as low as 43.1 percent according to statistics from the National Center for Education Statistics (Klein, 2015). Additional projections include 29.9 percent of students will be Hispanic, a gain of four percentage points since 2014; while the percentage of black students will hover at a near steady 15 percent (Klein, 2015).

Looking at the teaching population, 80 percent of current teachers are white, and that number is holding steady – even through the 2023 predictions (Klein, 2015). These statistics are alarming as several studies show the importance of students being taught by educators of similar race and/or ethnicity as they serve as role models (Klein, 2015). A 2014 report from the Center for American Progress echoes these statements saying that when students see teachers of color they view them as role models and believe the school to be more welcoming (Boser, 2014).

Principals who wish to ensure that students from diverse ethnic backgrounds are welcomed at school and are able to learn must hire teachers who mirror their population. Often these teachers have "insider knowledge" (Boser, 2014, n.p.) and can relate better to students from similar backgrounds and of similar color. The same can be said for students from differing countries. For immigrant students, it is vital that interpreters and English language educators are available to translate and help with forms, homework, and classwork. Events and bulletin boards that showcase the countries of the student population, special events, and traditions will create a culture that values diversity.

Students from Poverty

The landmark Coleman report of 1966 was the first to verbalize that an economically disadvantaged student has more barriers to learning at school than a student from a more affluent family (Sparks, 2016; Alexander & Morgan, 2016). The report concluded that integration was key to raising up poverty-driven students, and that families were "key drivers of student achievement" (Sparks, 2016, n.p). Over time, black students have made gains in reading and math; yet, their progress is not equal to that of white peers (Sparks, 2016). Another startling fact is that the staff in urban schools often do not often represent the student population with the majority of the workforce having identified as white (Sparks, 2016; Alexander & Morgan, 2016). Finally, motivation and mindset, or an academic growth mindset, were seen to be higher in more advantaged groups of students than those from poverty (Sparks, 2016).

The National Center for Poverty released statistics from 2016 that showed 41% of all children under 18 years of age were living below the poverty line although the percentage was actually four points less than it was in 2010 (Koball & Jaing, 2018). Children of immigrant parents are more likely to come from homes below the poverty line than natural-born students, while children whose parents work part-time are more likely than their peers to be from low income or poor homes (Koball & Jaing, 2018).

Families in which the parent has a high school degree or less than a high school degree were more likely to struggle financially, while some college ensured a degree of financial safety (Koball & Jiang, 2018). Finally, single parent homes struggled the most with 69% living below the poverty line; while almost half of the families who were poor or low-income received some assistance from the federal Supplemental Nutrition Assistance Program, known as SNAP (Koball & Jaing, 2018). With these statistics in mind, school leaders are tasked with ensuring basic needs are met so that students are able to access learning without the stressors of poverty (Jensen, 2013).

According to Jensen (2013), there are seven factors that are tied to socioeconomic status that affect the students' ability to engage in active learning to include (1) health and nutrition, (2) vocabulary, (3) effort and energy, (4) mindset, (5) cognitive capacity, (6) relationship building, and (7) stress levels. Students who lack the socioeconomic status to achieve these factors come to school with a lack of focus and an inability to access the curriculum. It is up to the principal, therefore, to engage the appropriate school staff to help students and families find resources that can assist in solving both the immediate problems and long-term poverty issues.

Mitigating the socioeconomic issues is a time consuming and difficult task. Ensuring students have access to breakfast and lunch while at school as well as the school nurse will help ensure the first factor is addressed (Jensen, 2013). Engaging families in discussion and giving them a better understanding of how to speak with and work with their child at home can assist with factors such as vocabulary, cognitive capacity, mindset and effort and energy (Young, Jean, & Mead, 2019). Connecting families and community services can often decrease stress levels in both the student and the family, which, in turn, gives students the feeling of safety they need learn (Young, Jean, & Mead, 2019). Although the reality requires a long-term solution, short term fixes can make the difference for students who fall below the poverty line.

Students with Disabilities

Students with disabilities between the ages of 6 and 21 number upwards of 5.8 million as of the fall of 2014; and this is up from a low of 5.6 million in 2011 (Samuels, 2016). Students with specific learning disabilities such as dyslexia have the greatest share of the population at 39% of all students identified (Samuels, 2016). These numbers underscore the importance of ensuring that educators are prepared to teach students whose needs may differ from their peers.

Principals are tasked with providing all the necessary ingredients to help teachers and students find success despite differences among the academic needs of diverse learners. The most recent learning disabilities (LD) study completed by Horowitz, Rawe, and Whittaker (2017) suggests areas to specific to LD that must be considered; yet they can be broadly applied to all areas of special education by principals as a means to ensure academic compliance for everyone. The categories include (1) understanding the issues, (2) identifying struggling students, (3) supporting academic success, (4) considering social, emotional, behavioral challenges, and (5) transitions after high school.

Understanding the issues. There are myriad disabilities that require students to need assistance of one kind of another. Principals cannot be expected to know them all; yet they must have a clear picture of their student body and what the students need to succeed. Having a well-trained educational team leader, 504 coordinator, school adjustment counselor, content specialists, intervention teachers, and classroom teachers can assist in determining how best to help the students in the school.

Identifying struggling students. Students from poverty, of color, or English language learners are more likely to be diagnosed with a specific learning disorder; yet disabilities can happen to anyone. Teachers must be vigilant when assessing students using formative and summative assessments, as well as quick checks, as a means to identify students who would benefit from further assistance.

Principals must ensure that staff have worked through a teacher/student/parent assistance team and used a multi-tiered system of supports as well as specific interventions prior to requesting a 504 or IEP evaluation (Horowitz et al., 2017). Students may have a variety of disabilities that require either a 504 or an IEP, and each either make accommodations to the work or environment or modifies the work or environment, respectively.

Supporting academic success. Whether students require a 504 or an IEP, or simply need in-class accommodations, supporting academic success may include a pull-out or inclusion setting with special education teacher or paraprofessional support, small breaks, or extra time, to name just a few. Knowing what each child needs to be successful is the job of the special education team and classroom teachers. In students with specific learning disabilities, statistics show the importance of 'just-right' academic interventions as 90% of students with SLD scored below proficient on the 2013 National Assessment of Educational Progress (NAEP) (Horowitz et al., 2017). Students with a 504 were more than twice as likely to be retained as were 85% of students with an IEP and on average (Horowitz et al., 2017). Alarmingly, 71% of students with a 504 or IEP did not make it to high school graduation (Horowitz et al., 2017).

In order to improve these statistics, the study suggests that reading interventions for struggling students be a primary consideration, IEPs should include high standards and measures of success, and educators should utilize universal design for learning as well as other personalized learning features to improve student success rates and academic outcomes (Horowitz et al., 2017). These fall under the purview of the principal who is responsible for ensuring that educators have the professional development and observation/feedback loops regarding academic content and delivery to put these practices into action.

Considering social, emotional, and behavioral challenges. Chronic absenteeism is higher in students with disabilities due to medical appointments, frustration, social maladjustment, emotional struggles, and behavioral issues that lead to suspension (Horowitz et al., 2017). Students with disabilities are twice as likely to be suspended as compared to their peers, three times more likely to drop out prior to graduation, and one-third more likely to be involved with the justice system (Horowitz et al., 2017).

To combat these issues, principals are encouraged to expand early screenings, focus on social-emotional learning as a foundation for academics, engage and empower families early and often, cultivate educators through professional development and preservice teaching programs, and enforce civil rights laws as they pertain to the school and its students (Horowitz et al., 2017).

Transitions after high school. High school students with disabilities are more likely to struggle after graduation if they do not have resiliency skills and are not able to advocate for themselves (Young, Michael, & Citro, 2017). For this reason, high schools should ensure students have been taught self-advocacy skills and that they are confident and self-aware (Young, Michael, & Citro, 2017). Internal resiliency includes having a positive temperament and using the accommodations and strategies offered in 504s and IEPs (Horowitz et al., 2017). College students with disabilities are less likely to self-identify, at only 24%, while 76% did not inform the college and instead struggled or believed they no longer had a disability (Horowitz et al., 2017). Students who chose careers after high school were twice as likely to be jobless as compared to their non-disabled peers (Horowitz et al., 2017).

In order to prevent college and career dropouts, high school principals must ensure that students receive counseling and training in resiliency and self-advocacy skills, and transition planning (Young, Michael, & Citro, 2017). The federal government has several acts in place to bolster young adults with disabilities in both the post-secondary and work settings. The RISE Act of 2016, which stands for respond, innovate, succeed, and empower, requires institutions of higher education to accept 504s and IEPs as evidence of a learning disability when presented to the disabilities office on campus (Horowitz et al., 2017). Career-bound graduates with disabilities have more opportunities than ever before due to newer federal legislation that includes the Workforce Innovations and Opportunities Act of 2014 as well as several other mandates.

Final Thoughts

Fostering a positive school culture through an equity lens requires the principal to consider the needs of all staff and students and find solutions that benefit each student individually. Principals who ensure that educators mirror the student population and that teaching practices differentiate for student need and ability will be on the road to a school in which all are valued.

Transformational leadership is at the heart of a positive school culture. Here, principals are forming trusting relationships, encouraging collaborative practices and decision-making, helping staff to make meaning of situations and policies and, in turn, the staff rallies and becomes a more cohesive unit. This is the basis for a school in which teaching and learning are paramount and students come first.

Due to the differences in urban, suburban, and rural communities, equity is not always a reality. Urban areas, and sometimes rural areas, traditionally have a higher rate of poverty and low tax base, which then reduces the per pupil funding available. This is in stark contrast to suburban settings where poverty levels are low, and a high tax base provides a setting in which schools and principals are better able to provide for their students.

Other considerations in fostering a positive school culture through equity and inclusion include ensuring a supportive learning environment for students from diverse backgrounds, students with disabilities, students who are gender diverse and of diverse sexual orientation, and students of poverty. Each has a differing set of circumstances and needs that require unique interventions and equitable practices. Principals who can help educators think inclusively will ensure all students receive a more equitable experience. This open thinking and respectful environment improves the culture in a school and leads to improved student outcomes.

Points to Remember

- *At a minimum, principals interested in fostering a positive school culture must consider the responsibility of the teaching community to equitable practices, a teaching population that mirrors its students, and policies and practices that ensure equity in learning.*

- *Equity and equality are not the same. Equality is the same treatment with similar resources, while equity is treatment tailored to the needs of each student and full access to resources.*

- *Transformational leadership fosters a positive school culture through trusting relationships and collaborative decision-making. Principals who lead in this way undertake change in small increments, explain proposed change and why it is good for the learning community, help staff to make meaning, and have more staff buy-in.*

- *School leaders must consider the needs of students from diverse backgrounds, those who are gender diverse, students with disabilities and those who come from poverty. Student need must take precedence and a principal who uses an equity lens will naturally be more sensitive to full inclusiveness.*

Chapter 8

Tapping Technology: Standards and Instructional Practices with Promise

In recent decades, technology has become a necessary tool for administrators, educators, and students alike. From each vantage point, virtual tools offer a new lens from which to view management, teaching, and learning. Educators are asked to teach using technology and virtual tools, while students are required to complete tests, search for information, and practice academic standards from myriad content areas – all from the screen placed before them. It is the administration, however, who is responsible for finding the 'just-right' devices and tools, as well as creating the conditions that allow these to be implemented with fidelity and confidence.

In 2009 the International Society for Technology in Education (ISTE) released a set of standards for administrators that set the tone for a "technology-rich learning environment" (n.p.). Recently, however, ISTE has released a new set of administrator standards, along with a name change – ISTE Standards for Education Leaders - that has the ability to transform any school into a technology hub full of possibility (The International Society for Technology in Education, 2018c).

In addition to administrator standards, school leaders are asked to use software for many day-to-day tasks that were once completed on paper or by phone. Observations, evaluations, as well as data collection and analyzation, are all tasks that now benefit from a technology twist. Equally helpful, mass calling tools and a variety of social media platforms create easy access and allow for two-way communication with families (Baskwill, 2013; West Corporation, 2018).

Moving beyond administrator tasks, there are hardware and software options that can change the way digital natives learn as well as the way that educators teach. Hardware options include interactive whiteboards, laptops and tablets, while there are myriad software programs available for content area and soft skills (Cauler, 2014; Miller, 2017). Universal design for learning, the SAMR model, and Project Based Learning, all have valuable ties to technology-rich, integrated learning (CAST, 2018a; Walsh, 2015; Larmer, Mergendoller, & Boss, 2015). Administrators must consider not only what will be taught, but also how it will be taught. With so many options, it is important to dissect each and how it has changed the job of the school leader.

Standards for Administrators

The International Society for Technology in Education (2018a) believes that technology has the ability to "transform teaching and learning, accelerate innovation and solve tough problems in education" (n.p.). Through their conferences and writings, they aim to inspire solutions that will "improve opportunities for all learners" (The International Society for Technology in Education, 2018a, n.p.). These impressive goals led to the creation of essential conditions, and then standards for educators, students, coaches, computer science teachers, and education leaders (The International Society for Technology in Education, 2018a).

Essential Conditions

ISTE created a list of 14 conditions, replete with definitions for each element that they believe are critical to the leveraging of technology as a means for learning to occur (The International Society for Technology in Education, 2018b). ISTE (2018b) also created a diagnostic tool that can be used to determine the existing weaknesses and strengths in a school or district as well as help to create and implement an action plan based on the collected data (n.p.). The ISTE (2018b) essential conditions list includes

- Shared vision: leadership, along with all stakeholders must agree on a focused vision for educational technology
- Empowered leaders: leaders at all levels are empowered to lead the change
- Implementation planning: shared vision and logical planning of all digital resources, information, and communication technologies
- Consistent and adequate funding: budgets reflect the shared vision and implementation needs by allocating financial resources
- Equitable access: connectivity must be reliable for all stakeholders, all the time
- Skilled personnel: leaders and educators are able to select appropriate technological resources based on the needs of the student body

Tapping Technology

- Ongoing professional learning: professional development must be continuous and focused, and stakeholders must be given time to practice new skills
- Technical support: all technology users have access to tech support in order to keep both hardware and software in good working order
- Curriculum framework: all academic standards, as well as the specific technology standards, are aligned with the resources available
- Student-centered learning: all teaching is based on student need and ability
- Assessment and evaluation: all tools and assessments must be evaluated for best fit on a regular basis
- Engaged communities: community partners are valued, and relationships developed and maintained by academic leaders
- Support policies: all policies and financial planning support the use of technological tools and digital resources
- Supportive external context: federal, state, and local initiatives support policies and schools with implementation and continuous learning

While the list is long, each condition helps to set the stage for a successful implementation of technology for the specific task of student learning. In addition to the essential conditions, education leader standards help to leverage technology and all the components necessary for successful student and teacher outcomes.

Standards for Education Leaders

The five standards for educational leaders offer administration at all levels a roadmap from which to plan and lead the work of ensuring technology-based learning (The International Society for Technology in Education, 2018c). Each standard looks deeply at what is needed to reframe learning using digital tools and student-based learning. Using the five standards helps school leaders integrate educational technology and meaningful learning into a new and exciting academic process that engages students at all levels (The International Society for Technology in Education, 2018c). What follows is a brief overview of the new standards:

Standard 1: Equity and citizenship advocate. This standard reminds leaders that technology must be used to "increase equity, inclusion, and digital citizenship practices" (The International Society for Technology in Education, 2018c). Leaders are tasked with ensuring that (1) qualified, tech savvy teachers are in each classroom, (2) access is available to all students equally, (3) leaders are evaluating resources and digital tools for high quality as well as modeling acceptable discourse, and (4) promoting digital citizenship for students and teachers (The International Society for Technology in Education, 2018c).

Standard 2: Visionary planner. Leaders establish a strategic plan that includes a vision, mission, and evaluation cycle with all stakeholders that promotes "learning with technology" (The International Society for Technology in Education, 2018c, n.p.). The importance of this standard is that it provides a cyclical process for evaluating progress towards the larger goal of using technology as a tool for students to use in all realms of education and as a means to increase student outcomes. As a visionary planner, the leader is tasked with learning from, and sharing with, other leaders who are on the same or similar quests (The International Society for Technology in Education, 2018c).

Standard 3: Empowering leader. School administrators are tasked with ensuring that all stakeholders are "empowered to use technology in innovative ways to enrich teaching and learning" (The International Society for Technology in Education, 2018c). As part of this standard, administrators build up the skills and confidence of those around them as a means to employ the ISTE Standards for Students and the ISTE Standards for Teachers (The International Society for Technology in Education, 2016; The International Society for Technology in Education, 2017). The culture created by the empowering leader is such that a digital culture where innovation, collaboration, and exploration is valued and revered. Here learners of all ability levels can improve their academic prowess and social-emotional needs are met (The International Society for Technology in Education, 2018c).

Standard 4: Systems designer. This standard aims to provide a secure and safe environment, while ensuring the infrastructure is strong, and the strategic plan implemented with fidelity. The cyclical nature of this work lives in the knowledge that resources and needs will be ever-changing and students and teachers will always need updated supports, technology, and digital tools to stay on the forefront of student achievement.

Standard 5: Connected learner. For a school leader to ensure a technology-rich school, it is vital that professional development is continuous and focuses on "emerging technologies for learning, innovations in pedagogy and advancements in the learning sciences" (The International Society for Technology in Education, 2018c). For this reason, administration must participate in learning that supports new innovations, technologies, and digital tools. Equally important, using a growth mindset at all times will ensure learning communities that value technology and all it has to offer student-centered learning and vice versa (Kazakoff & Mitchell, 2017).

These standards set the tone for a school leader's work. When examined and put into action, the standards for administrators ensure a clear path to a technology-rich environment ripe for student-centered learning and improved student outcomes. This occurs through hard work, a team approach that involves all stakeholders, and a belief that cyclical assessment will provide the continual improvement needed for a diverse and ever-changing student body.

Ensuring the Technology Needs for Teachers and Students

The school leaders' role in driving technology as a means to more involved learning must include a specific set of criteria to ensure success. Similarly, the ISTE standards for both educators and students are important tools for implementation of a technology-rich academic setting (The International Society for Technology in Education, 2016; The International Society for Technology in Education, 2017). The educator standards offer a roadmap that includes learner, leader, citizen, collaborator, designer, facilitator, and analyst; while the student version includes empowered learner, digital citizen, knowledge constructor, innovative designer, computational thinker, creative communicator, and global collaborator (The International Society for Technology in Education, 2016; The International Society for Technology in Education, 2017). Some similarities and/or overlap exists, and this is intentional as educators and students in technology-rich, student centered classrooms and schools often share the roles of facilitator and learner (CAST, 2018a).

As school administrators begin to look towards these new and improved classrooms, it is imperative that staff are prepared and understand the SAMR model, universal design for learning, and Project Based Learning (Walsh, 2015; CAST, 2018a; Larmer et al., 2015). In their own way, each of these additions to the teaching/learning process will increase technology integration and student learning. They must first be taught through professional development; however, educators then need time to hone their skills and should be given actionable feedback to improve their practice.

SAMR Model

Originally described by Puentedura, the four steps of this model provide a linear map to technology implementation and integration in the classroom (Walsh, 2015). The four steps, substitution, augmentation, modification, and redefinition can be split into two equal parts along a continuum. The first two simply enhance technology and its integration into the classroom, while the second two steps are more transformational and completely change the way in which students learn new content as well as changing the educator into the facilitator (Young, Jean & Citro, 2018).

Substitution might be trading out paper and pencil for a word processor, while augmentation would add in a speech to text option to the substitution model (Young, Jean, & Citro, 2018). Modification occurs when students share documents created during the augmentation stage. Once shared, students might offer feedback and reflective thoughts for the student authors. During the redefinition stage, students create a completely new task that was never dreamed of previously and then share with a global audience where it is vetted, and feedback is given for reflection (Walsh, 2015). This dovetails nicely with Project based Learning and sharing of the final product.

All stakeholders will benefit from the SAMR model, and it is vital that school leaders, educators, and students must make their way to redefinition as quickly as possible if they are to embrace a technology-rich and integrated classroom (Young, Jean, & Citro, 2018). School leaders and staff need to become early adopters, trying new and different technologies and digital tools as quickly as possible in an effort to ensure they can guide student scholars towards independent learning situations.

Universal Design for Learning

Universal Design for Learning (UDL) is a tool used to ensure that inclusive learning communities are a central part of learning (CAST, 2018a). Through well-articulated principles that guide the design and implementation of personalized lessons, UDL looks at the why, what and how of learning (CAST, 2018b).

Multiple means of engagement: The 'why' is directly related to motivating students through purposeful engagement. Educators who engage students in the 'why' of learning, create motivated and purposeful learners (CAST, 2018b). Educators must (1) find what interests the student, while minimizing distraction, (2) mix-up the activities to prevent boredom and foster collaboration, and (3) provide expectations that push students while not alienating them and create self-assessment tools as a means of personal reflection (CAST, 2018b)

Multiple means of representation. The 'what' relates to representation and acknowledges that learners have a variety of ways to present information that shows they are knowledgeable and resourceful learners (CAST, 2018b). Here educators are responsible for (1) finding alternate ways to present information in both the visual and auditory realms, (2) clarifying, supporting, promoting, and illustrating language and symbols in such a way that students see just-right options, and (3) ensuring comprehension through options such as activation of background knowledge, highlighting information, guiding the process as needed, ensuring generalization (CAST, 2018b).

Multiple means of expression. The 'how' is through differentiation; this is both the action and the expression of learning. Students who engage in the 'how' of learning tend to be goal-directed and strategic learners (CAST, 2018b). This important final step requires educators to (1) ensure assistive technology and navigation, (2) provide multiple tools and media as well as ensure tiered supports, and (3) guide, support, facilitate, and enhance options for executive functions (CAST, 2018b).

School leaders must ensure that educators are well versed in UDL as a way to create engaging, personalized lessons using just-right features. Once educators are trained in UDL, they must use it daily and receive timely, actionable feedback to ensure they are following the tenets with fidelity.

Project Based Learning

When implemented correctly, Project Based Learning, or PBL, is a rigorous, extended opportunity for students to dive into authentic, real world problems (Young, Jean, & Citro, 2018). Using both prior knowledge and the inquisitiveness of searching for new knowledge, students find solutions that lead to mastery of skills and deep understanding of concepts (Larmer et al., 2015).

Recently renamed Gold Standard PBL in order to correct learning gaps from the original concept, teaching practices and two matching circles, each provides guidance on proper implementation (Larmer et al., 2015). The first circle, essential project design elements, are critical to ensure that the project maximizes student engagement and learning, while the inner circle, student learning goals, focus on skill development as well as academic content (Larmer et al., 2015). The teaching practices guide educators to become facilitators who help students find the answers for themselves (Larmer et al., 2015).

Essential project design elements. To maximize student engagement and learning, educators must include seven elements into the project to include a challenging question or problem, sustained inquiry, authenticity, student choice and voice, reflection, critique and revision, and public product (Larmer et al., 2015). Leaders would be wise to ensure that these components are clear in lesson plans and visible during walk-throughs and observations. Actionable, detailed feedback is essential if the educator is to master PBL.

Student learning goals. While the goal is for students to be successful learners and have meaningful life experiences, PBL professes that this happens through content knowledge and skill development (Larmer et al., 2015). Two key skills are vital for students to attain when working on projects; key knowledge and understanding as well as key success skills (Larmer et al., 2015). Key knowledge and understanding concepts and standards that all students must know, yet here they are applied to real world issues. Key success skills are typically called college and career readiness skills and include problem solving and critical thinking skills. Combined, these lead students in the direction of success.

Project based teaching practices. Similar to the other two components, teaching practices consist of seven elements to include design and practice, align to standards, building culture, managing activities, scaffolding student learning, assessing student learning, and finally, engage and coach (Larmer et al., 2015). While these appear to be traditional teaching practices, Gold Standard PBL tweaks them to help educators facilitate learning instead of being the "sage on the stage" (Larmer et al., 2015).

Hardware and Software Options

While most districts create and implement a hardware plan for laptops, tablets, and such, and they often provide the learning management system, it is not unusual for school leaders to use school-based funding to support the purchase of interactive whiteboards and digital tools (Miller, 2017). More often than not, older students have smart phones, and these can also be powerful learning tools. Many schools have a 'bring-your-own-device' (BYOD) policies in place; however, if the appropriate digital tools and hardware are not in place, it will not matter what is purchased for a school or what the school leader hopes to accomplish (Miller, 2017)

Interactive Whiteboards

First introduced in 1991, an interactive whiteboard has become a must-have tool in every classroom as a way to develop "fundamental skills for any student" (Lee, 2017, n.p.). Whether mounted or moveable, whiteboards act as a classroom screen where videos from the internet can be shown, where specialized software allows for students to write directly on the screen while projecting, or where a finger functions as a mouse and/or pen while working on content from any number of academic areas (Lee, 2017).

Classrooms with interactive whiteboards boast several benefits including, lessons that are structured to meet the needs of a diverse student body, a more enjoyable learning process, students and teachers who are more engaged in the learning process and with each other, revision and review of material learned, and better visuals and audio helps students with disabilities access the content taught (Hutt, 2017). School leaders also appreciate the reduced hit to the supply budget as chalk, erasers, pencils, and paper become less important (Hutt, 2017). The online classroom also benefits from interactive whiteboards in that they provide more flexibility bringing in students from all over to attend to one lesson (Hutt, 2017).

As proof as to the difference between classrooms with and without interactive whiteboards, students appear to be more engaged in the 70% of primary and secondary schools that have this tool (Lee, 2017). Not only that, those same students show greater engagement, higher attendance rates, and better grades (Lee, 2017). It would appear that this multisensory tool is a proven gold mine for student learning.

Learning Management Systems

A learning management system (LMS) is similar to "a brick and mortar schoolhouse with a variety of rooms, each with a different purpose" (Young, Jean, & Citro, 2018). Each room houses a different application – student growth, school operations, teacher empowerment, parent engagement, and so on. An LMS is usually chosen by the district dependent on the needs of their stakeholders; however, principals must be able to access and use the system in such a way that makes their job easier. Brightspace and PowerSchool are two examples of learning management systems that have the ability to ensure educators can post grades, assess students, use learning tools that promote student growth, and engage families, while other features include personalized professional development, educator evaluation, and recruitment and hiring options (D2L, 2018; PowerSchool, 2017). The right LMS can do just about anything the school leader needs in order to run a school.

Digital Tools

Myriad digital tools exist to improve the educational experience of students. Many of these applications, or apps, engage students and prod them to complete learning tasks they may otherwise have avoided. While many of these apps have no empirical evidence to prove their educational worth, they offer students differentiated instruction and mastery of content (Vaala, Ly, & Levine, 2015).

Digital learning tools. Digital apps such as i-Ready and IXL provide lessons targeted at several content areas that are aligned with the Common Core standards (Curriculum Associates, 2017; IXL Learning, 2018). These game-like lessons are adaptive and meet students where they are, make content relevant, and close gaps (Curriculum Associates, 2017; IXL Learning, 2018). Educators become empowered with real-time data, student performance indicators, and personalized professional development (Dreambox Learning, 2018).

Several of these apps can be predictors of future student outcomes on high stakes testing (Curriculum Associates, 2017).

Other digital learning tools, such as Discovery Education, incorporate educational functions such as digital textbooks and streaming along with personalized professional development (Discovery Education, 2018). Mystery Science and StemScopes are science specific and New Generation Science Standards (NGSS) aligned (National Science Teachers Association, 2014; Mystery Science, 2018; Accelerate Learning, 2018). The creators of StemScopes include a downloadable section on PBL (Accelerate Learning, 2018). They provide educators with lesson plans, videos, literacy development, assessments, and inquiry-based personalized instruction.

Word processing tools. Products such as Office 365 offer educators and students a plethora of options for collaborative work, individualized learning, and making connections (Microsoft, 2018). Students and educators can collaborate or provide spaces for personalized learning using tools such as Teams, Word, PowerPoint, and Class Notebook (Microsoft, 2018). Google Docs offers real-time collaboration as several individuals can work simultaneously on one document (Techopedia, 2018).

Social Media

There are myriad social media options that school leaders can use to connect to families. Often, school districts provide a website with individual school "pages" where postings include important dates, a calendar, recent photos, blogs, v-logs, and other items (Stribbell, 2014). Some districts promote Instagram, Twitter, or Facebook, while others shy away and prefer to keep their own pages. Monitoring each site is essential so that the school leader is aware of any potential issues as well as positive press (Stribbell, 2014).

Regardless of the vehicle, visitors must be able to sense the culture of the school and understand the commitment to students and families (Baskwill, 2013). For the school leader, communicating with families is paramount and social media is a vehicle that, due to smart phone use, lends itself to the cause. Communication must be two-way, and responses should be given in reasonable time frames as the 21st century has become very instantaneous. The National School Public Relations Association is quick to remind principals and other school leaders that social media can "assist in strategic messaging...especially in a crisis situation" (Hood, 2014, n.p.).

While only a few of the many options available to the field of education have been explained, it is easy to see that multiple and often overlapping programs can meet the needs of a diverse student body and educators whose abilities are in different places along the SAMR continuum (Walsh, 2015). The job of the school leader, then, is to ensure the programs and tools chosen match the needs of the school population and that those needs are evaluated and examined regularly to ensure the digital tools are still appropriate.

Final Thoughts

The principal has myriad responsibilities within the school and ensuring a technology-rich environment is just one of them. In the 21st century, it might be argued that it is the most important one due to advances in teaching methods, diverse student bodies, and digital natives and their families who prefer this method of learning. The convenience of a single access point for all required tasks ensures that time is well spent.

The ISTE standards for education leaders offer a comprehensive five-point framework that considers the components necessary to ensure a technology-rich, integrated school where all students have access to personalized learning (International Society for Technology in Education, 2018c). Combined with the essential conditions and standards for both educators and students, this powerful collection will take districts, schools, leaders, teachers, and learners to the next level of digital education (The International Society for Technology in Education, 2016; The International Society for Technology in Education, 2017).

Putting the standards into action, the visionary planner must provide the appropriate technologies, put them in place, train educators and give them the time to practice their craft. Securing a cyclical evaluation process provides a way to make mid-course corrections, while communicating with all stakeholders turns educators and others into leaders as well. Technologies are ever-changing, and it is imperative that school leaders use a growth mindset to consistently improve the teaching and learning that is within the school.

Technology has become a significant part of education and, as such, it behooves the principal to carefully reflect and then select the appropriate tools to connect staff, students and families, while engaging students in meaningful and creative learning processes. Using the SAMR model, universal design for learning (UDL) and Project Based Learning (PBL) all create the conditions for more student-centered learning to occur (Walsh, 2015; CAST, 2018a; Larmer et al., 2015). By its very nature, this is personalized learning that uses technology to create educational products that have meaningful components and that were student made through deep understanding and mastery of knowledge.

Learning management systems, digital tools, and social media all play a part in the creation of a technology-rich, integrated school. It is vital that principals provide two-way communication to families who are also connected to social media. While some tools and technologies are district mandated, others are at the discretion of the school principal and can be based on the needs of the staff and students. Interactive whiteboards ensure a learning space that can be used as a larger than life laptop, to show online materials, and/or to connect with others.

Principals have been tasked with school management using technology, educators have been asked to teach with technology, and students are expected to learn using technology. It is, therefore, imperative to create the conditions and choose the appropriate tools to ensure that management, teaching, and learning can occur with fidelity, so that the outcome is well-rounded, deep thinking, creative college and career ready students who can go into the world with confidence.

Points to Remember

- *ISTE standards for education leaders include equity and citizenship advocate, visionary planner, empowering leaders, systems designer, and connected learner. These five elements provide the basis for technology integration in schools (International Society for Technology in Education, 2018c).*

- *The fourteen ISTE essential conditions are research backed and provide a roadmap to "guide implementation of the ISTE standards, tech planning and system wide change" (International Society for Technology in Education, 2018b).*

- *SAMR, universal design for learning (UDL), and Project Based Learning (PBL) are tools that educators should use to ensure a technology-rich classroom environment where the student is the gatherer of knowledge and the teacher is the facilitator. Educators must be trained and have time to hone these skills in order to transfer them to the students.*

- *An interactive whiteboard is an important learning tool that offers students and educators myriad options. Students and educators can use their finger as a pen or a mouse on the large screen and they can watch movies and other media that brings learning closer.*

- *Learning management systems, social media, and digital tools all provide access to technologies that improve the learning conditions when used properly. This includes two-way communication that is vital to keeping families informed and involved in the school.*

Chapter 9

Your House or Mine:
Meeting Families at the Front Door

Families come to school with personal attitudes and beliefs that may be foreign to principals; as such, preconceived notions may arise regarding why parents who don't show up for school events, a disregard for families whose primary language is not English, and many others. These false beliefs lead principals to assume families are unreachable or don't have the capacity to engage with their child's learning (Lendrum, Barlow & Humphries, 2013; McKenna & Millen, 2013). It behooves school leaders to examine and capitalize on parents' assets and the wealth of knowledge families have about their children to create family-school partnerships that are deep and meaningful (Parr & Vander Dussen, 2017).

The Importance of Family-School Partnerships

Family-school partnerships are important to the education of children as they support academic and social needs in school, increase attendance, and lead to higher graduation rates (O'Donnell & Kirker, 2014). Families who are engaged with their children's learning and schools realize important pay-offs such as proficient reading abilities, better math skills, higher grades, better employment after high school, and an increase in pay as compared to peers whose families are not involved (O'Donnell & Kirker, 2014). In one study on family engagement, "higher levels of family involvement participation significantly and positively predicted better student social skills and work habits" (O'Donnell & Kirker, 2014, p. 222).

In order to have effective engagement programs, understanding parents from their earliest experiences is significant. Research findings by Miller, Dilworth-Bart and Hane (2011), "underscored the importance of understanding parents' educational histories in order to better understand children and highlights the types of memories that may be most lasting and influential for mothers as they prepare their children for school" (p. 161). Minimal research has been completed on how parents' experiences during their own developmental years influenced their intent to engage with their child's school; yet, understanding parental histories and how personal history influences parents' behaviors of engagement in their child's school is a phenomenon that continues not to be well understood or researched (Raty, 2011).

A 1994 landmark publication was recognized and used throughout school districts for many family-school engagement programs (Henderson & Berla, 1994). Henderson, Mapp, Johnson, and Davies (2007) have been actively involved in recording data on family-school engagement and its impact on student achievement and effective practices that support it for more than more than thirty-five years. More recently, researchers such as Henderson et al. (2007), Epstein (2018), Mapp and Kuttner (2014), as well as Grant and Ray (2016) have been instrumental in redefining and reshaping the types of parental engagement and the system that would support engagement in schools for all families.

In 1995, the *Epstein Framework of Six Types of Involvement* was developed and has been used consistently by PTA organizations to define practices that encourage family engagement (Epstein, 2018). Mapp, whose movement in the early 2000s focused on what was needed for families to be engaged with their children, continued to push for including parents in decision-making processes in schools and active engagement (Mapp, 2010). As these concepts began to gain more traction in the field of engagement, the federal government and corporations began to take notice of the positive links between families, schools, and higher graduation rates (Duncan, 2014).

Historical perspectives

Family engagement policies and procedures have long been a requirement of school improvement plans. As far back as the Civilization Fund Act of 1819, policies dictated family engagement be directed at middle class families until President Lyndon B. Johnson argued that all families need to be given opportunities to be integrated into schools and that families of color be included as well (Baquedano-Lopez, Alexander, & Hernandez, 2013).

The Elementary and Secondary Education Act of 1965 further focused educational goals on families living in poverty. In 1991, the Coleman report cited families losing interest in their child's schooling due to work demands and the beginning loss of the nuclear family; however, the 2001 reauthorization of the ESEA under NCLB worked to build bridges between home and school (Grant & Ray, 2016).

The former No Child Left Behind Act (NCLB), and the current Every Student Succeeds Act (ESSA), both require state education agencies (SEAs) and local education agencies (LEAs) to have written plans (Hirano & Rowe, 2016). On the school side, under ESSA, Title 1 schools must have parent and family engagement monies set aside (Hirano & Rowe, 2016). Historically, family-school engagement initiatives have been influenced by "perceptions of parents' backgrounds and of the roles expected of them by school administrators and teacher" (Baquedano-Lopez et al., 2013, p. 150) however; Valencia (2010) would argue that this approach uses deficit thinking.

Terms Changes Over Time

The concept of 'family involvement,' was redefined by Ferlazzo in 2011 to that of 'family engagement.' Using the dictionary as a guide, Ferlazzo (2013) noted that "involve is to 'enfold or envelope,' whereas one of the meanings of engage is 'to come together and interlock.' Thus, involvement implies *doing to*; in contrast, engagement implies *doing with*" (Ferlazzo, 2013, p. 10). This change in terminology was the jumping off point for those in education who wanted to engage families in a new kind of partnership that valued relationship building as the cornerstone to student success (Mapp, 2010).

A great deal of work has been completed to strengthen family-school relationships in just a few short years. Most recently, the U.S. Department of Education released the Dual Capacity-Building Framework for Family-School Partnerships, which was a joint collaboration between the Federal Department of Education's Family and Community Engagement Division and Karen Mapp (Walsh, 2014). This project and subsequent document carefully delineated the "systemic processes around family-school communities" (Young, Jean & Mead, 2019).

Schools use a variety of definitions of family engagement and have chosen to implement a variety of strategies and tools for family engagement practices. Federal legislation around Title I advocates for School-Family Compacts; however, this practice tells families what is expected and does not develop partnerships. This practice "misses the policy goal of shared responsibility and partnership" (Baquedano-Lopez et al., 2013, p. 155) and explains that the achievement gap is not caused by students but rather by economic disparities and racial oppression.

Under ESSA, recruitment for family–school partnerships must include every parent and family member (Klein, 2016). No longer is the term engagement aimed solely at parents, rather it now considers the entire family including extended family members and those not necessarily related but who, in some way, are in charge of the student's education activities. Family-school compacts are now designed jointly together and involve all family members. Furthermore, building school capacity includes community and business leaders and those who affect families (Henderson, 2016).

Understanding Families' Stories

Stories are the fabric that holds families together; they are traditions passed down from one generation to the next. Retold by those who have lived experiences, stories are about what we know and who we are; in other words, they define "us" (You et al., 2016). They describe and help those around them understand the human phenomena about their lives. Linked together like a quilt, each patch tells a life story, the trials and tribulations, and the good and bad regarding human existence.

Many families who tell their stories have come to the United States for a better life; yet some tales do not have happy endings. Many of the stories include topics such as "duality, loss, longing, triumph and contradiction, some by choice and coercion" (Donnella, 2016). As immigrants tell their stories, "they push beyond fairy tales and there is a stark difference between expectation and reality" (Donnella, 2016, p. 2). There is great difficulty in packing up and moving to an unknown land; families must learn new customs and cultures, how to navigate schools, the medical field, and shopping in a world that may seem hostile (Sargent, n.d.).

The role of the principal is to stop and listen; realizing that leadership must provide a path for them and for their dream of a life in the United States. As leaders, our interpretations of the stories are vital to understanding the families past experiences, where they have been successful, and where they have struggled (McKenna & Millen, 2013). Listening with empathy and heart helps to understand the nuances the story is telling, while asking questions for clarification is warranted to ensure understanding.

Though relating similar experiences may seem to aid the conversation, many times it leaves the storyteller questioning the ability of the listeners understanding of the experience (Mead, 2017). The principal is tasked with being authentic and acknowledging that the family story is most important. It is not up to any one single person to agree or disagree with what the family has said - especially if it is controversial or outside of the listener's experiences; rather, it remains important to listen and seek to understand. Many stories may not be in the listener's realm of knowledge; however, walking in their shoes while being told the story will help the educator become better versed about their experiences to learn how it informed the family's beliefs and values (Mead, 2017).

As an example, a family recently came across the border. The mode in which they traveled, the amount of money they paid to get them there, and the conditions they endured were concepts the leader could not relate to; yet their eyes as they told the story, the strife and difficulty the family had endured while in transition to join their children (Mead, 2017). The parents showed a true sense of relief that they were now in the United States; yet fear remained with them. By understanding the trauma the family shared, the leader was better able to assist, providing a more welcoming and integrated school experience.

School administrators must think about how these fears are transferred and manifested in their children's lives.

- Would the children live in fear daily?
- What would the emotional fallout look like and how would they manifest in the classroom?
- What behaviors could the leaders change to help make them feel safe in the schools?
- These are all considerations that the principal must develop into action plans.
  (McKenna & Millen, 2013)

Though family stories will assist in understanding the lived experiences parents have had, underlying factors may become evident as they transverse their child's school. In another story, the family shared that their parents never had any communication with their schools, did not attend parent meetings, or participate during group activities; rather, the parents worked hard at educating their children at home about respect and religion while they understood that schools were responsible for their academic education (McKenna & Millen, 2013; Mead, 2017). An invisible cultural boundary separated school from families and had been maintained through many generations. It was necessary, then, to look at the areas of education that could be offered to help families develop more skills to engage in their child's school.

Implementing the Dual Capacity Building Framework for Family-School Partnerships

The Dual-Capacity Building Framework for Family-School Partnerships document provides educational entities with a compass of process and organizational conditions, and policy and program goals to support active family-school partnerships (Duncan, 2014). This hallmark framework also provides schools with a solid foundation to embellish their family-school partnerships while the demographics of their populations become more inclusive of families from all over the world (Duncan, 2014). Schools that implement this framework report a systems change that increases parent engagement and student achievement, especially for those who are from immigrant families (Mead, 2017). Under ESSA further work is mandated both on the state and local level to even the playing field for all families by bringing equity of opportunities to be engaged in partnerships that support student learning and success (Klein, 2016).

Implications for Practice

There are eight areas of recommendations for schools hoping to increase family-school partnerships as well as strategies for teachers, schools and parents seeking to increase student academic achievement through greater engagement. The Every Student Success Act (ESSA) (Klein, 2016), a federal act that replaces the No Child Left Behind Act, requires that school-family partnerships be redefined and specific interventions must be implemented in each district to build capacity for families, teachers and the community. As guided by the National Association for School, Family and Community Engagement (2016), school districts must:

- Offer assistance to parents in understanding the education system and the state standards, and how to support their children's achievement;
- Provide materials and training to help parents work with their children;
- Educate teachers and other school staff, including school leaders, in how to engage families effectively;
- Coordinate with other federal and state programs, including preschool programs;
- Give parents information in a format and language they can understand; and
- Provide reasonable support that parents may request.

The joint policy statement from the U.S. Department of Education and the Department of Health and Human Services (2016) clearly outlines recommendations for national, state, and local early childhood systems development on family engagement. Based on the assumption that "family engagement promotes children's learning and healthy development" (U.S. Department of Education and the Department of Health and Human Services, 2016, p. 1), the document delineates the steps needed to develop systems that are inclusive of all families "integrated throughout systems and programs, and that families are essential partners in providing services" (U.S. Department of Education and the Department of Health and Human Services, 2016, p. 1). Both the ESSA and the above policy statement serve schools as tools in the development and improvement of their family, school, and community engagement systems and initiatives.

The Dual Capacity-Building Framework for Family-School Partnerships serves as a compass for school districts in their development of family-school partnerships. Research confirmed the use of what they termed as process conditions to engage families (Mapp & Kuttner, 2014; Gillanders, McKinney, & Ritchie, 2012). Process conditions are:

> a series of actions, operations, and procedures that are part of any activity or initiative. Process conditions are key to the design of effective initiatives for building the capacity of families and school staff to partner in ways that support student achievement and school improvement. They must be linked to learning, relational, developmental, collective/collaborative and interactive (Southwestern Educational Development Laboratory [SEDL], 2013, p. 9-10).

The Dual Capacity framework provides strategies for growing the competencies of teachers, staff, and parents by simultaneously building their four C's: capabilities, connections, confidence, and cognition (SEDL, 2013). When schools and parents work and learn collaboratively, the results will be partnerships that have all the ingredients necessary to support children to become successful learners (Duncan, 2014; Mead, 2017). The framework also further defines the best possible approach to learning about new families either by inviting them to their child's school or making a home visit.

The family-school framework addresses ways to mitigate many of the negative experiences expressed by families through their stories. Changing policies and forming culturally relevant and inclusive procedures enables educational institutions to be more welcoming by recognizing the capital of families (Mapp & Kuttner, 2014). Establishing a culture of listening to family's stories will enhance partnerships. When administrators step outside of their role to that of learner, they will be able to appreciate each story and the expertise each family brings to schools (SEDL, 2013). As principals begin to recognize the rich cultural capital that families have, the more cultural responsiveness and appropriate interactions will result (Mead, 2017).

Though there are endless strategies being implemented by school systems across the United States, the Policy and Program Goals section of the Dual Capacity-Building Framework are the most important in increasing parents and staff capabilities, amalgamating beliefs, and building self-efficacy (Mapp & Kuttner, 2014). The goals promote collective capacity learning for both educators and families. In order for partnerships to be developed, there needs to be a clear understanding of the funds of knowledge both partners have. Recommendations for educators and families are grouped into the four areas as defined in the Dual Capacity-Building Framework for Family-School Partnerships, those of capabilities, connections, confidence, and cognition (SEDL, 2013).

The word partnership takes on many meanings at different levels for educators, schools, and families. In the best of worlds, partnerships mean fair and equitable participation in decision-making at the school, district, and community level (SEDL, 2013). For many families, partnerships may remain simply showing up at school events, attending open houses, and parent-teacher conferences. Principals who understand their stories and who concentrate on meeting parents where they are most comfortable will be able to increase partnerships.

Capabilities

Capabilities are the skills and knowledge that the community possesses that support engagement. These skills include cultural competency, ways to build trusting relationships, advocacy skills, language acquisition (Mapp & Kuttner, 2014), and other skills necessary to support families' development. For some school communities the capabilities of families are strong, whereas other school communities need further improvement and development to strengthen them (Mead, 2017).

Recommendation #1: Increasing Knowledge of Teachers

Professional development for teachers. Recommendations for building strong schools and the capabilities of school staff, teachers, and parents include professional development on developing family-school engagement, cultural competencies, and understanding themselves as teachers from a cultural approach. Most educator preparation programs provide minimal coursework on building family-school partnerships (Mead, 2017); therefore, it is pertinent for existing educators to become proficient in this subject area.

From a systemic approach, building first-year teacher knowledge about the importance of family-school partnerships requires teacher preparation programs to include coursework on partnership strategies. Globally changing college-level curriculum content to include understanding the philosophical approaches to engagement and developing strategies that incorporate working with diverse populations is required. Using Mapp and Kuttner's (2014) four C's to build content is critical to strengthening education programs that will help schools and teachers understand the importance of school-family partnerships.

Training in cultural competencies, goal setting and implementation. School administrators at the central office level usually work under the goals of the superintendent, policies set forth by governing boards, and a district engagement or family-school partnership plan. Often, it is the plan developed for Title 1 schools. Trainings focused on cultural competencies, understanding diverse families, setting short and long-term goals, and implementing policy change are required to build strong systems throughout their schools (Vilson, 2015). Training that includes developing family-school partnerships is often a pivotal point for school districts (Redford, 2017). By creating a shared vision for engagement by both parties, schools can identify changes required to increase family-school partnerships.

Individual schools, their principals, teachers, and staff must cultivate ways to build their knowledge of families within their school (Reedy, 2014). Professional development that includes brainstorming strategies to understand and include diverse families is vital. Smaller districts may be able to implement a district-wide plan whereas larger districts may choose to implement an overall plan with strategies that are customized to and make the most sense for their particular family population (Vilson, 2015).

Recommendation #2: Increasing Knowledge of Parents and Families

Hosting community conversations. Ways to build human capital at the school level include hosting community conversations, led by trained facilitators in a safe environment. The community conversation is used to enhance education, solve issues, and answer questions through a respectful, constructive, and collaborative process that is conducive to empowering schools and families (Legeros, 2016). A conversation topic is solicited by the community or chosen by the facilitator. The outcome of the conversations is to build a better understanding of the issue and solutions through interactive education and discussion. Meeting the predetermined goals for the conversation and follow-up are important to continue building skills of the participants and to build lasting partnerships that increase trust within the community.

Increase English as a second language classes. Increasing adult education classes delivered through various platforms and offered at times convenient to participants improve the ability to be engaged. Han's (2012) study validated that as parents acquire skills they increase their language competency. In this study, participants saw the value in linking with others who had better language ability to help overcome senses of helplessness. Class offerings that accommodate parents' working schedules or childcare needs are best utilized. It is suggested that these classes be held at times and days that are convenient for parents with childcare provided. Offering activities in the early morning and late evening hours or weekends as well as at multiple locations are beneficial.

Support for language acquisition. Support for families to overcome language barriers through continued attainment of language skills increases their ability to converse in English. Families that have the ability to speak and understand languages is critical to being engaged and is a skill that needs to be constantly practiced under the leadership of a person with higher skills (Mitchell, 2016). Ongoing support groups led by trained facilitators increases discussions of issues that are important to parents and ultimately build their conversation skills in their non-native language. Being able to understand each other helps define and clear up any misperceptions and creates meaningful dialogue that results in more engagement (Mitchell, 2016).

Understanding schools and their systems. Immigrant parents want to understand how schools in the United States work, what their systems are, and how they benefit their children. Facilitated discussions by school leaders or family liaisons about the multiple systems within schools can be broken down by sections and explained to families (Mitchell, 2016). Helping families understand the specifics of the special needs system is paramount to being able to work collaboratively. Understanding systems helps families recognize how their cultures may be alike and/or different and learn ways to acclimate to American systems (Mitchell, 2016). Schools can offer their own workshops on navigating special education systems or can partner with agencies that offer the training.

Recommendation #3: Meeting Families Where They Are

Accommodating working schedules. The lack of attendance at school events caused by parents' working hours has been a concern shown by teachers. Often parents have to work two jobs to put food on the table and pay for living expenses; therefore, they can't attend daytime meetings. Many parents may have negative feelings toward schools when teachers infer that parents don't care because they don't attend school events, rather parents' working schedules impede their attendance at events. Offering activities in the early morning, later evening hours, and on weekends as well as multiple activities that engage families at different levels is beneficial (Nunez, 2017).

Addressing families' comfort levels. Activities directed at different comfort levels of families and alternative locations outside of the school boundaries are important for all families seeking to build their skills (Nunez, 2017). Literacy home parties fashioned after direct marketing parties have been significantly successful in some districts, as families feel comfortable in each other's homes (Young, Jean, & Mead, 2019). One parent invites other parents and their children to his or her home, as well as their school principal, literacy leader, or family liaison. They read during the party with their children in a relaxed atmosphere while learning strategies to increase vocabulary, reading skills, and family networking skills. The families leave with new books to increase their home reading library.

Recommendation #4: Creative Ways to Engage Families.
For families, specific training about what children are learning in their classrooms, how schools operate, and how to advocate for their child and larger school issues (e.g., lack of funding), is valuable. Family camp offers education and activities for parents and their children. This 'un-conference' is facilitated by trained discussion leaders on various topics, around large round tables with parents, teachers, staff, community members, and administrators (Hernandez-Prados, Garcia-Sanz, Parra, & Gomariz, 2017). It pulls from the expertise and perspective of the participants through collaborative face-to-face conversations, resulting in shared experiences and further education about what is best for their children. The discussion groups are 45 minutes to an hour in duration, and in a morning's time, participants can experience three to four topics of their choosing.

Other more formal trainings that use research- and evidence-based curriculums include Parents Supporting Education Excellence (PSEE) created by the (CT Center for School Change (2018). During the courses, participants have the opportunity to learn about schools, what families can expect and how partnerships might be formed as well as strategies that can be used to increase student practices that lead to greater achievement (CT Center for School Change, 2018). The graduates have gone on to be active members of school governance councils, PTA, and other leadership groups.

Advocacy training for change. To enhance family and schools' capabilities, there are outside organizations that have substantial advocacy training available and special education organizations that specialize in issues that understand special education requirements and advocate for children with special needs. Other trainings support parents in understanding civics and social responsibility that result in a community project and can often be completed within a school by addressing an issue of concern or need within the school. Throughout the training, participants learn to set rules and procedures that support collaborative relationships.

Connections

Connections focus on social capital in schools, families, and communities and how these strengths create safety nets for schools and families. Connections build social networks and relationships that are built on trust and respect. "These networks include family-teacher relationships, parent-parent relations and connection with community agencies and services" (SEDL 2013, p.

10). Ideally included in the connections are "efforts to better connect robust early childhood systems to the elementary schools" (Jacobson, Rollins, Brown & Naviasky, 2016, p. 28).

Recommendation #5: Changing Behaviors for Better Relationships and Communication

Often parents feel that teachers didn't want to change their behaviors toward parents, as it means extra effort to secure translations of written materials and interpreters for meetings. When teachers and school institutions focus on what is best for the child and take the extra steps to ensure services that families need, parents develop better connections that are vital and have lifelong, lasting effects for engagement (Grant & Ray, 2016). Though there may be deep-seated beliefs by both families and teachers, these negative feelings can be changed into positive ones by having multiple possibilities to engage between the two. Consequently, schools that provide multiple engagement opportunities will see a higher level of family-school partnerships and fewer parents who feel helpless. Changing behaviors of both parents and teachers will go a long way to improving the relationship between them, resulting in students and families who are more fully engaged in school and have higher graduation rates.

Assesses family knowledge. Families' views of themselves can develop into cohesive partnerships when fears of intimidation are eliminated. Often, families new to the United States are cognizant that their ability to speak English is poor, that they don't understand American systems and their capacity to build relationships is minimal; however, families play multiple roles that are linked to their child's learning: parent, self-learner, guide, and mentor (Nunez, 2017). Schools that assess what families know, understand their strengths and areas that they want to develop, what they would like to learn about, and what activities they enjoy, will find this information valuable to building relationships.

Dedicated time for relationship building. Building relationships that afford parents a sense of being well connected with their child's school is perhaps the biggest challenge for educational institutions. With other priorities competing for a spot in one's daily calendar, dedicating time to building family-school partnerships is often an afterthought or an add-on; hence, schools that have dedicated time for building relationships see more parents connected to their child's school (Mapp, Carver, & Lander, 2017). Strategies such as implementing advisory boards that ask for parent input and feedback establish better relationships. Schools that hold 'coffee with the principal' or other small group activities are vested in hearing from parents who begin to feel treasured by their child's school (Mapp et al., 2017). Parents then begin to view authority figures as wanting to help by sharing their teaching expertise to help parents and families understand their child's education system.

Authority. Respecting authority is paramount to all parents as they raise their children. Parents often speak about respecting school authority; however, at the same time, it made them feel fearful and intimidated. When schools share the authority by building relationships with their students' families, the result is shared authority and decision-making (Grant & Ray, 2016). Two-way respect between teachers and parents enable asking questions and clarifying academics. Parents then feel comfortable, welcomed, and respected as part of the family-school partnership.

Changing daily interactions when children go to kindergarten. Continual connectedness of the parent to the child's educators and school is paramount to building and maintaining school-family partnerships. Through daily interactions in preschool, families and programs build wonderful family-school partnerships that support their child's learning. The degree of interaction often drops when the child goes to kindergarten (Kostelnik & Grady, 2009). Due to families dropping off and picking up their children from early childhood programs, daily dialogue is easy; unfortunately, these interactions decrease at kindergarten unless schools make concerted efforts to maintain the level of conversations.

One strategy to maintain contact includes using a communication notebook (Fiorvanti, 2015). These are especially valuable with children who may be identified as needing more services on a daily basis. Teachers and therapist share the child's daily activities, concerns, and any questions with the parent in writing, while the parent writes in the book about the child's activities at home, eating, sleep habits, and other concerns (Fiorvanti, 2015). Daily or weekly phone calls or emails are always appreciated especially when the contact is giving families praise about their child.

Daily communication and the use of technology. Helping families feel connected to schools takes hard work and consistent bi-directional conversations that build confidence and trust (Baskwill, 2013). Bi-directional text messages are seen as a valuable communication tool for use; especially when the technology platform is in multiple languages (West Corporation, 2018). Parents who experience this type of communication feel connected to their child's school and that the teacher cares about their child; therefore, parents are more open to asking questions and raising concerns.

Communication with the community. Communication plays a large role in helping families and the community-at-large to develop confidence and trust in its schools. Conversations that ask for ideas from the community and act upon them in a timely basis build confidence in their schools. Inviting community stakeholders to be part of decision-making processes is a lengthy yet a high impact strategy. On-going conversations that occur year around, and not just at budget time, help builds confidence in the leadership's ability to perform their jobs. When the community and its stakeholders have confidence in its schools, they become engaged in activities and projects that support diverse learners to become successful (Baskwill, 2013).

Recommendation #6: Integrated Approaches through Cross Community Collaborations.

Families who feel a sense of connectedness to the community in which they live "feel more confident in their role as parents" (U.S. Department of Health and Human Services and the U.S. Department of Education, 2016, p. 4). The old adage 'it takes a village to raise a child' becomes evident. When communities provide integrated approaches through cross-collaboration of agencies, families are able to obtain services that support their families' development and build their social networks. Service providers that become trusted by families are aware of their own cultural competencies to meet a diverse community and are most valued by the families.

Another side of connections is that of the community's trust toward its schools. Without trust, connections cannot be made to support school success. With increased diversity in school populations and higher expectations of student testing, the community will either continue to support its schools or develop a lack of trust in its schools in educating its children (Hanover Research, 2016). In today's trying times, superintendents, administrators, and teachers must make every effort to continue a dialogue on the challenges and successes of student achievement, and what strategies are in place to build achievement, and elicit the community-at-large to support initiatives that are being undertaken to increase achievement (Hanover Research, 2016).

School events that invite families and community members for collaborative discussions about the challenges it faces and, where goals are decided by consensus, help build trust and confidence in their schools. Goal-focused community collaborations made up of social service agencies, service providers, schools, higher education, and businesses are valued commodities and build the wealth for its families, students, and schools. An initiative such as StriveTogether (2018), a cradle-to-career model, solves social problems by bringing together community resources to develop one goal-focused organization pertinent to the needs of that community. Successful StriveTogether (2018) partnerships are evident in sixty-eight communities across thirty-two states in the United States.

School-based services inspire trust and increase family knowledge. Other smaller initiatives are individual community initiatives that encompass service providers often led by community-based organizations (Barnum, 2018). School-based services such as family resource centers or family learning centers offer playgroups for young children under the age of five and their caregivers. These services begin to unite families before their children go to school by connecting families to one another while they enjoy educational activities during children's first five years of life. Trainings are for parents on topics to include, but not limited to, educational issues, understanding Common Core Standards, and what parents can do to support and enhance instruction at home, and provide transitional activities as families move to kindergarten and through other grades (Common Core State Standards Initiative, 2018).

Parent Teacher Home Visits. Originated in California, parent teacher home visits stop assumptions and implicit bias that educators and family members may have about each other (McKnight, Venkateswaran, Laird, Robles, & Shalev, 2017). Home visits in which teachers listen to families discuss first their dreams and hopes for their children, rather than academics, is paramount to developing positive relationships. After the relationship evolves into a family-school partnership, only then is academics discussed (McKnight et al., 2017). Developing the relationship first before academics lessens power struggles between parents and educators. By understanding each other first by learning about each other promotes positive partnerships.

Creating connections with families with young children, the mindset of parents and the community changes to reflect the value of early learning and family engagement, resulting in schools that value family-school partnerships by employing strategies that are inclusive (McKnight et al., 2017). The connections then become part of a unified community initiative that support families with children from cradle to career.

Confidence

Parents with a sense of comfort often have enough self-efficacy or confidence in their skills and abilities to help their student with schoolwork, participate in school events, and be knowledgeable about decision-making processes.

Recommendation #7: Development of Parents' and Families' Self-Efficacy

Families with enriched social networks are comfortable and engage in skill-building to develop their self-efficacy. Building parents' ability to communicate and engage in partnerships, schools and families learn how to work across lines of cultural differences (Mapp, 2010). Schools that ensure that all family engagement is culturally relevant and respectful, that curriculum and learning are reflective of all cultures, and that there is sufficient availability of interpretations, help families assure that schools care. Building a sense of comfort with schools includes teachers knowing the make-up of the families in the class and what contributes to making schools welcoming and inviting. Being welcoming includes institutional behavioral changes through personnel training and conscious changes to the school's physical and cultural environment (Mapp, 2010).

Building skills through adult education. Learning skills pertinent to what children are learning can be integrated into adult classes, resulting in parents who are effective in assisting their children with their homework. Gaining more knowledge about Common Core standards and strategies to use at home enables families to develop self-efficacy that they are part of the school community and are working towards common goals (Common Core State Standards Initiatives, 2018).

Use of interpreters. Interpreters play an important role in meetings, conferences and events that help build parents' knowledge of what is going on in their child's school (Mathewson, 2016). Parents may have the knowledge already, yet the language barrier is an issue to understanding the content of the conversation. Including an interpreter in the conversation when necessary builds further trust and caring between parents and the schools. When parents are seated in the main area of a presentation and interpretation is done simultaneously, parents feel less separation than those parents who are moved to another part of the room. More expertise with modern technology should be employed for interpretations and further studies on practical ways to increase communication when there is a difference of languages is beneficial (Mathewson, 2016).

Cognition

Cognition refers to the beliefs, values, and views that schools, families, and the community contribute to partnership. Schools, families, and the community must be devoted to understanding cultural differences and similarities and believe in the values of having diverse partnerships.

Recommendation #8: Schools Assess Parent Beliefs and Values, and Create an Action Plan

Schools assess the core beliefs of administrators, teachers and staff. Schools must assess and discuss the core beliefs and values of administrators, teachers, and staff around family-school partnerships, how they are linked to supporting families and student learning, and what strategies are most valuable, by setting up a plan of action to develop positive partnerships. Districtwide values must illustrate "a commitment to family engagement as a core strategy to improve teaching and learning" (SELD, 2013, p. 26).

Families and schools that learn to work in harmony by taking steps to realize their vision take on the role of change agents. The change agents, in most cases, have also been through cultural training to examine value and belief systems, and have engaged in advanced coursework that provided a clear foundation of what successful family-school partnerships look like.

Cultural considerations. Many families new to the United States can't assimilate and change their beliefs and value systems quickly enough to be fully accommodated and accepted into American culture. In many cases, however, when children come to the United States, their parents hadn't had the opportunity to internalize new values and beliefs; thus, they were not able to help their children acquire new cultures, and those cultural barriers remained (Vilson, 2015).

Educators with knowledge of different cultures have remedies ready to help families in their enculturation process, and proficiency in transitions are able to help families with their assimilation into American schools. Educator and staff training on different cultures and supporting different cultures have been valuable in schools. Bringing parents into small discussion groups where they are willing to share their culture with others is valuable. Educators who appreciate different cultures might ask a parent to present to the class or in small groups about their culture.

Perceptions and assumptions. It is suggested that educators be able to determine and talk about their perceptions and assumptions about family-school partnerships (McKnight et al., 2017). Recognizing perceptions and assumptions help educators learn about their own social and knowledge capital about families to build partnerships on a strength-based model. Educators who acknowledge and cherish parents as their child's first teacher overwhelmingly embrace parents' success (Mapp, 2010). The advantage of building partnerships on families' strengths is that engagement can be built using parent's funds of knowledge.

Importance of connecting adult learning to student goals. Regardless which of the four C's that schools and families choose to undertake, they should be considered as a package and not stand-alone parts; the content of the instruction needs to focus on student learning. Parents who walk away without any knowledge of how new skills relate and impact what their student is learning, don't necessarily see their importance in the educational process. When adult instruction is linked to what the student is learning, and life-long skills are embedded in the instruction, parents see the importance of such engagement and look forward to the next opportunity to build their knowledge (van Voorhis, Maier, Epstein, & Lloyd, 2013). Math and literacy nights, for example, are valuable, high impact approaches to improve academic performance.

What Else Can Be Done?

Formalized evaluations that gauge the school climate and inclusiveness of a school may use a team approach to evaluate the school environment from its physical characteristics to staff, educator, and administrator behaviors (Human Rights Campaign Foundation, 2018). Other attributes such as a warm and welcoming bilingual school secretary and the features of the physical building impact how parents feel toward their child's school. Removal of barriers helps boost a family's confidence in the system including having native-speaking school staff that helps assimilate families, such as family liaisons. Having family resource centers and specially designated staff responsible for family-school partnerships builds more relational trust, respect, and confidence. When families feel welcomed and integrated into their child's school, they are more willing to take on leadership roles in PTOs and decision-making opportunities in school governance councils (Human Rights Campaign Foundation, 2018).

Final Thoughts

Family dynamics are changing. Families want to be active in decision making regarding their child's academic career, yet they may not know how to access the educators or school in a viable way. The role of the principal is changing to reach out to families where they are and find creative ways to work with them. The Dual Capacity Building Framework for School Family Partnerships is the compass that most schools across the United States are implementing to engage families. It is time that principals and educators think about changing their beliefs and values systems to a new paradigm; that of realizing the strengths all families possess and instead of thinking that families will come to school doors, to thinking about creative ways to meet families where they are at their door.

Points to Remember

- *It is essential that principals and school leaders realize the strengths that families have and develop creative ways to engage with them.*
- *Educators' understanding of where families have traveled, what barriers they have faced, and their beliefs and values that they possess are heightened when they are able to listen to the stories of their families.*

- *Stories offer cues as to how schools and teachers might work with families in ways that are more inclusive and understanding.*
- *The Dual Capacity Building Framework for Family-School Partnerships is a nationally recognized compass for principals to use in developing the competencies of both families and educators.*
- *All families do not have the knowledge to navigate schools; thus, it is vital that principals and schools find a creative way to meet families where they are comfortable to increase family-school partnerships that ultimately increase school graduation rates.*

Chapter 10

The Importance of School Law: Positive Outcomes for All Students

Prior to 1965, schools were largely segregated, and education was delivered to students based on the color of their skin. The government had not yet weighed in on the necessity of providing equal education to all, regardless of nationality, race, gender, or ability. Academic demands were at the discretion of the city or town via the school board and families rarely questioned the methods used. More than fifty years later, federal laws direct districts and school leaders in most aspects of the educational requirements and needs of students.

As far back as 1896, the Supreme Court ruling of Plessy v. Ferguson stated that segregated facilities that were equal in space and contents were legal; and students attended schools based on race (A&E Network, 2018). It was not until 1954 and the Brown v. the Board of Education Supreme Court decision that determined that separate but equal was, in fact, not equal at all, and that public schools were required to provide access and education to all students (A&E Network, 2018). Taking school desegregation one step further, the Supreme Court decision of Runyon v. McCrary in 1976, stated that private, nonsectarian schools could not deny admission based on race (A&E Network, 2018).

Within this same timeframe, Lyndon B. Johnson began the "War on Poverty" (Social Welfare Project, 2016, n.p.), believing that by offering high quality equal education to all, poverty would be eliminated. It was then that the original Elementary and Secondary Education Act of 1965, and its subsequent versions to include the No Child Left Behind Act of 2001 and the Every Student Succeeds Act of 2016, were authorized (Klein, 2016). The federal government gave funding to states in return for requiring them to increase academic success for all students, especially those affected by poverty, through specific mandates (Klein, 2016; Social Welfare Project, 2016).

In similar fashion, two United States District Court cases framed the need for federal mandates to protect students with exceptionalities. In 1971, Pennsylvania Association for Retarded Children (PARC) v. the Commonwealth of Pennsylvania was heard by the United States District Court for the Eastern

District of Pennsylvania and ruled that students with intellectual and learning disabilities should be evaluated and placed in publicly funded schools that best met their needs (University of Kansas-School of Education, 2018). In that same year, the district court heard Mills v. the Board of Education of the District of Columbia and ruled that equal educational opportunities must be granted to students labeled as exceptional, to include those with behavioral issues, learning disabilities, and mental deficiencies (University of Kansas-School of Education, 2018).

These court cases led to a congressional quest to determine the magnitude of infringement of rights for students with disabilities. The Bureau of Education for the Handicapped investigated and found that there were approximately 8 million children who required specialized services in 1972 and just under half were receiving adequate schooling (University of Kansas-School of Education, 2018). Of the remaining students, 2.5 million received a "substandard education and 1.75 million weren't in school" (University of Kansas-School of Education, 2018, n.p.). Three years later, the Education for All Handicapped Children Act of 1975 was signed and provided further guidance specifically to protect and educate students with exceptionalities (Lee, 2018; U.S. Department of Education, 2007). Four times since the original bill was signed into law, amendments have created a stronger, more equitable vision of educational equality.

In addition to these considerations, principals must keep in mind constitutional laws that pertain to the school such as the first and fourth amendments, and specifics such as school finance and student discipline. It is vital that principals understand the history behind laws that affect the educational well-being of students and staff, as well as the intent of each law, in order to work with families and protect the students and staff they are tasked with serving. Only through a thorough understanding of federal laws that have a direct bearing on education, can principals influence the academic and social direction of the school in a way that honors the past and creates well-rounded, academically strong, students for the future.

Understanding Education Reform

Elementary and Secondary Education Act

The year 1965 saw a change in public education as the federal government passed the Elementary and Secondary Education Act (ESEA). This collective set of mandates attacked poverty and provided equal access to education across the US; theoretically closing the achievement gap between children who lived in poverty and their peers who were more advantaged (Social Welfare Project, 2016). ESEA funneled educational monies to states to be used specifically for instructional materials, support for educational programs, professional development of educators, and the development of family engagement activities (Social Welfare Project, 2016).

ESEA was divided into six sub-provisions, each with a specific focus area.

- Title I distributed varied amounts of funding to school districts based on the percentage of low-income and poverty-stricken families within each state and district.
- Title II funded preschool programs, school libraries, and the purchasing of textbooks.
- Title III supported additional educational programming when traditional school was not in session as well as special education services in rural areas.
- Titles IV allocated monies for educational research and training.
- Title V set aside money necessary to supplement grants.
- Title VI set the limitations and definitions as they related to ESEA. (Social Welfare Project, 2016)

At various times since its inception, ESEA has been reauthorized – each time changing with the differing beliefs of the president in office and the needs of the country at large. In 1969, for example, President Nixon included funding for low-income and refugee children, added to the vocational act, and established the Teacher Corps (Zascavage, 2010). The 1972 amendment included a sex-discrimination mandate, while the 1984 version included financial assistance to aid schools in meeting bilingual and English language instructional needs (Zascavage, 2010). The remainder of the 20th century saw substantial additions and changes to Title I, as those in power began to focus on school improvement and student achievement.

In 2001, the reauthorization of ESEA took shape in the form of the No Child Left Behind Act with a focus on increased accountability at the district and school level (Social Welfare Project, 2016). Schools were expected to make adequate yearly progress (AYP) and would face corrective action and restructuring if they fell short. Schools were also expected to post a report card that detailed demographics and student achievement outcomes. Finally, NCLB offered protection to at-risk populations and gave military recruiters access to high school juniors and seniors personal information (U.S. Department of Education, 2004). There were criticisms of NCLB, most notably that it caused states to lower their academic standards to avoid punitive actions by the federal government (Brenchley, 2015).

The latest version of ESEA was authorized in December of 2015. The Every Student Succeeds Act (ESSA) expanded the mandate for high quality preschool, invested in evidence-based interventions, required the sharing of information regarding district accountability and student progress, upheld protection for high-need, at-risk, and disadvantaged populations, and, for the first time, required student were taught using "high academic standards that will prepare them to succeed in college and careers" (U.S. Department of Education, n.d.a, n.p.; Klein, 2016).

ESSA offered more flexibility than in the past with changes regarding how states may use federal funding, how low performing schools are identified and assisted, and how educators will be evaluated (Klein, 2018). To ensure compliance, states were required to submit accountability action plans that needed approval by the federal education department. What happens next is yet to be determined; however, principals are at ground zero to enforce the state and district goals in an effort to comply with federal mandates.

What Principals Can Do

The National Association for Elementary School Principals (NAESP) created an interactive tool that outlined an action plan meant to help principals find success in interpreting and implementing ESSA (National Association for Elementary School Principals [NAESP], 2017). In addition to offering resources and suggestions on engagement with state leaders, it reviews and offers actionable ideas for each of seven topics to include standards and assessment, accountability, school improvement, district Title I resources, professional development, student support and academic enrichment, and high-quality preschool (NAESP, 2017). NAESP believes that these are the keys to a "well-rounded and complete education" (NAESP, 2017, n.p.). This includes a focus on student-centered learning, developmentally appropriate environments, high quality opportunities, and an aligned PK-3 curriculum that sets the stage for college and career readiness later on (NAESP, 2017).

Engagement and discourse. Engaging with state and district leaders is necessary as principals move forward to implement the tenets of ESSA. School leaders must intimately understand the requirements and expectations of ESSA so that they can lead their school in a positive direction with the whole child at the forefront of the learning process. To do this, they must be willing to discuss what a well-rounded education means and what a complete educational vision actually looks like on paper as well as in action; thus, a communication plan is important as is a focus on advocacy and tool development and implementation (NAESP, 2017). The principals who are most involved in the creation of ESSA policies at the state and district levels will surely see the greatest results within their own school.

Challenging content standards. NAESP suggests that principals work with district and state administrators to ensure that there is a comprehensive, challenging, and aligned body of content standards. This can be accomplished through a shared vision using ESSA specific language and through the development of an assessment system that is fair and balanced (NAESP, 2017). Using formative tools, Project Based Learning, and performance tasks will offer students hands-on experiences that show the value of learning not drill and kill for the sake of the test (Killion, 2012).

Accountability measures. While student outcomes are still considered to be important, ESSA offers states the chance to determine their own accountability measures (Klein, 2018). States must use a minimum of four indicators, yet this flexibility means that states can use items such as academic achievement testing, English language proficiency test scores, student growth in history/social studies or humanities, and/or a school quality or student success measure (NAESP, 2017). School quality or student success measures include, but are not limited to, items such as "kindergarten readiness, school climate and safety, student access to SEL opportunities, or student access to fine arts, foreign language, or other diverse learning opportunities" (NAESP, 2017, n.p.).

School improvement. School improvement is the third area of consideration and here principals are tasked with understanding and advocating for a well-rounded and complete education even in schools that require a turnaround plan (NAESP, 2017). The improvement plan must be grounded in research and use evidence-based supports, especially for schools with subgroups that are within the lowest 5% (NAESP, 2017). A needs assessment will direct the district in determining appropriate steps, and the principals should consider using monies for multi-tiered systems of support (MTSS) and preschool programming (Lexia Learning 2018).

Resources. Title I resources are usually of concern to principals and within ESSA it is no different. Districts must monitor student progress and meet state standards through the development of a comprehensive academic program (NAESP, 2017). Principals may have some flexibility in the programs offered at their schools, as well as how Title I monies are spent, although sometimes this is a district-based decision.

Professional Development. Specifically detailed in ESSA under Title II, professional development is the fifth of seven talking points for NAESP (2017). Addressing the learning needs of students, districts must have a specific plan of action that provides educators with focused and long-term learning and development that directly influences student outcomes. This is especially important in minority and low-income areas where the need for high quality teachers is profound (Parker, 2017). Funding can also be used at the discretion of the district or principal to fund peer interactions, gifted and talented programming, students and schools that suffer from chronic absenteeism, and specialized services for "students affected by trauma and mental illness" (NAESP, 2017, n.p.). Monies are also available to support grants and initiatives that support student needs in these areas.

Grant monies to support learning. A new grant meant to directly affect student support and academic enrichment can only be secured by states who are willing to complete a needs assessment, and then "promoting equitable access to the activities supported by the program" (NAESP, 2017, n.p.). Supported activities include the expansion of technology and other program conditions such as health and wellness initiative (Edutopia, 2018). For their part, principals should encourage superintendents to examine the grant and work to secure full funding in order to implement new programming at the school level (NAESP, 2017).

High quality preschool. The final indicator focuses on high quality early learning, something that the federal government has been promoting for quite some time, although the funding has been a source of frustration for cities and towns (NAESP, 2017). ESSA offers districts a chance to focus specifically on preschool through a concerted effort to expand access to services, align services and standards from birth to grade 3, and improve professional development and training for educators who "serve young learners through developmentally appropriate strategies and practices" (National Association of Elementary School Principals, 2017, n.p.).

This combination of engagement and understanding provides principals with a first-hand look and intimate knowledge of the intricacies and necessities of ESSA (Klein, 2018). If schools are to offer students a well-rounded and complete education, then it is up to the principals to determine school-based priorities within each indicator. NAESP (2017) echoes this sentiment and suggests that principals' leadership when working with state and district leaders will largely determine the "successful implementation of ESSA" (n.p.).

Understanding Special Education Reform

The Education for All Handicapped Children Act

Over forty years ago, several landmark decisions led to the creation of the Education for All Handicapped Children Act (University of Kansas-School of Education, 2018). Where once students who needed specific accommodations or modifications to access the curriculum received a sub-standard or separate education, or no education at all, the expectation was now for these students to be taught alongside their able non-disabled peers whenever possible (U.S.

Department of Education, 2007). During the years prior to the Education for All Handicapped Children Act, the government had laid a foundation that included developing specific protocols for students with disabilities; thus, by the time the act was authorized, educators had been trained to teach students with disabilities and these students were already being taught in preschools as well as elementary and secondary schools (U.S. Department of Education, 2007).

The overarching goal of the Education for All Handicapped Children Act of 1975 was to guarantee a "free, appropriate public education [FAPE] to each child with a disability in every state and locality across the country" (U.S. Department of Education, 2007). This included services and specialized education that met each students' unique needs, regular assessment and evaluation of the effectiveness of said education, to protect the rights of students and their families, and to offer states federal monies in order to ensure compliance under the law (U.S. Department of Education, 2007).

Over time, the law was improved and updated to better reflect the needs of students with disabilities. Where initially children did not receive services until they turned three years of age, an amendment in 1976 required states to offer services from birth and, in 1986, parents were given more rights to guide the development of their child's IEP (University of Kansas-School of Education, 2018). The 1990 and 1997 revisions of the law were substantial in nature and included new disability categories, an expansion of the age range from birth to nine for using the term "developmental delay," a requirement that students be exposed to the same curriculum regardless of ability, as well as mandated transition planning for post-secondary success (University of Kansas-School of Education, 2018). The 1997 amendment also saw a change in the name of the federal act - the Individuals with Disabilities Education Act, or IDEA (Lee, 2018).

The 2004 amendment included a shift in the required disbursement of funding, higher standards for special education teachers, early intervention, and "greater accountability and improved educational outcomes" (University of Kansas-School of Education, 2018). The latest amendments have been in response to the reauthorization of ESSA and include updated definitions, the removal and/or addition of guidelines, and the movement of some regulations (IDEA, n.d.).

Section 504 of the Rehabilitation Act of 1973

A civil rights law, the Rehabilitation Act of 1973 prohibits students with disabilities from being treated differently. While there are no federal monies attached to the statute, violators can have federal funding taken away (Council for Exceptional Children, 2018). The act was written in similar fashion to that of civil rights laws that protect minorities and women, yet the regulations to guide its use and explanation of terms had to be defined. It was not until a twenty-eight-day sit-in occurred in San Francisco, and shorter ones in seven other locations, that the regulations were passed with few changes (Cone, n.d.).

What Principals Can Do

As principals are at the ground level in ensuring the compliance of IDEA and 504 statutes, it behooves them to understand the laws that protect and educate students with disabilities and their families as well as to ensure compliance in order to improve student outcomes. As such, it is vital that both Parts B and C of IDEA as well as Section 504 are clear to principals and they are ready to act on behalf of their students. All principals should be well versed on the necessary steps to take when considering a 504 plan; or prior to, during, and after the IEP process that encompasses Part B of IDEA, which focuses on children aged 3 to 22 (Young, Jean & Mead, 2019). Some principals, especially those who have PK in their buildings, should also be familiar with Part C, which is specific to children birth to age 3.

Part C of IDEA. Laying out all the necessary steps that occur through early intervention, Part C of IDEA is a federally mandated process that finds, evaluates, and offers services to babies and toddlers from birth to age three who have disabilities or who have developmental delays or concerns (Young, Jean, & Mead, 2019). Families are also served in as much as they need to understand the issue and how to help their child. Early intervention focuses on the domains of physical, cognitive, communication, social/emotional, and self-help as a means to prepare young children for preschool and the future (Center for Parent Information & Resources, 2017; Young, Jean, & Mead, 2019).

Once a child turns three, they can attend public preschool in a least restrictive setting (LRE). LRE refers to the academic environment in which a student learns and according to IDEA, it must be with non-affected peers whenever possible (Center for Parent Information & Resources, 2017). Many children in preschool have transitioned from early intervention therapies and an Individualized Family Service Plan (IFSP) to an Individualized Education Plan, or IEP (Young, Jean, & Mead, 2019).

Families and children who were once serviced using early intervention, now find themselves starting over again with an education-only based plan. Principals who understand where their youngest students began, are better able to help their families acclimate to the rigors of public school as well help educators understand the needs of the student based on the IEP (Young, Jean, & Mead, 2019).

Part C of IDEA. For children aged 3 to 22, Part C of IDEA offers an educational plan that is on par with that of their non-disabled peers using accommodations and modifications. Once a student has been identified as needing special education services through testing, an IEP is created. During the meeting to determine eligibility, parents are asked to participate in a number of ways and principals should listen carefully so that they can reinforce school structures and federal mandates as needed (Center for Parent Information & Resources, 2017).

Educators trained specifically in how to teach and help these students are expected to carry out specific plans based on the requirements within the IEP. Principals would be wise to keep track of the number of students in need of services and check in with both their teachers and parents regularly, so that at the annual meeting to assess progress and review the IEP there are no surprises. In addition to the yearly meetings, students undergo a complete testing cycle every three years to assess the continued need for an IEP (Center for Parent Information & Resources, 2017).

Students who have more serious disabilities usually remain in the care of the school system until their twenty-second birthday. For these students, a transition plan is an important part of their final few years and principals must pay close attention to this process (Young, Bonanno-Sotiropoulos, & Smolinski, 2018a). The team, including the family, principal, special education teachers, and practitioners, are tasked with creating a plan for post-secondary success that may include post-secondary school or vocational training, community work, employment and/or independent living arrangements with or without support (Center for Parent Information & Resources, 2017).

Section 504. Schools are expected to provide reasonable accommodations that give students with designated handicaps equal access to learning, yet there are far fewer procedural and written requirements (National Low Income Housing Coalition, 2014). Students in need, according to the law, are those who have a mental or physical impairment that prevents them from participating in major life activities, yet they are of average intelligence (Council for Exceptional Children, 2018). Although the plan is written, there are no requirements as seen in the IFSP or the IEP process such as parent consent, instead, parents must only be notified (Council for Exceptional Children, 2018). Often students are taught in the general education classroom and may be given extra time or alternate location to complete testing, frequent breaks, or repeated directions. Principals are wise to know the specifics of this act, and how it differs from an IEP, so that they can answer questions that parents may have as well as help make determinations for a student who come up in review during Student Teacher Assistance Team meetings.

Understanding Constitutional Law

The US Constitution gives certain rights to students and staff that must be acknowledged. Some of these have been discussed in the context of special education as well as school reform; however, there are others that are specific to the operation of the school. These Constitutional laws may be written into the school district's student/parent handbook and/or the code of conduct.

The First Amendment safeguards free speech, and this allows students and staff to speak freely; yet there are limits within the bounds of public school in that speakers cannot "stand on a soapbox" (NCAC, 2013, n.p.), rather, it must pertain to the learning at hand. The First Amendment also covers censorship, or the lack of, for school protestors, social media, technology, and the school paper. In addition to free speech, the First Amendment has an establishment clause that dictates a clear separation of church and state and prohibits the display of religious symbols or practices in public schools (Longley, 2017).

The Fourth Amendment is search and seizure, and the Fifth Amendment is a due process; these are often used in combination, although, not always. The Supreme Court ruled that schools have the right to complete a search when probable cause is present (Bisk Education, 2018). As a next step, school leaders must convene a meeting where supporting details regarding the charges and the evidence can be explained, as well as allow the alleged perpetrator to tell his or her side of the story (Darden, 2006). The Fifth Amendment is also often used when fights or other offenses occur. It is often difficult to find the balance between school safety and students' rights, yet this is the task of the principal.

What Principals Can Do

In total, the Constitutional laws that affect public school students and staff are about personal freedom and protection. Principals can ensure this happens by creating both a culture and climate that are accepting of all people and respectful of all beliefs, while setting firm rules and expectations, and following the district code of conduct with fairness. When incidences do occur, it is important to ask for written reports, listen to all sides, protect each individual, and make decisions based on the Amendments and the district code of conduct. When this is the norm, principals become trusted problem solvers who find solutions that, while not all sides will like, everyone believes are fair.

Final Thoughts

At first glance school law may seem like it only pertains to special education. Ensuring educational freedom that honors a least restrictive environment, while giving students maximum support, is imperative. Understanding the nuances that lead to success in special education takes time and a principal must be willing to learn. Beyond this, all students deserve and are entitled to an equal education under the law. This includes not only academic aspects but those set forth by the Constitution as well. Freedom of speech, search and seizure, and due process are three very important considerations for principals. Each has a federal component as well as a school-based component and finding the sweet spot between the two is the place where school leaders must always reside.

Points to Remember

- *Several landmark federal court decisions influenced educational equality. The most famous was Brown v. the Board of Education of 1954, which stated that separate but equal was not equal at all and that all students, regardless of skin color, ethnicity, gender or ability, deserved the same education.*

- *The "war on poverty" as proclaimed by President Lyndon B. Johnson, included the Elementary and Secondary Education Act (ESEA) of 1965. The ESEA was divided into sections, called 'titles,' each of which described a different mandate, such as how to distribute funds to low income schools, how funding should be provided for professional development, grant monies available for programming, and high-quality preschool.*

- *The latest iteration of ESEA is the Every Student Succeeds Act (ESSA), which expanded preschool, included funding for evidence-based interventions, required greater district and school accountability, and higher academic standards.*

- *Principals can ensure ESSA by engaging with the state and district regarding the new regulations, ensure challenging content standards exist, push for greater accountability, follow the guidelines for school improvement, ensure professional development for all staff members, use grant money to expand school offerings, and ask districts for more preschool opportunities with high academic standards.*

- *The Individuals with Disabilities Act (IDEA), formerly called the Education for All Handicapped Children Act of 1975, required all schools that accepted federal funds to have free and appropriate education for all students, especially those with disabilities. The latest reauthorization included higher education standards for special education teachers, early intervention for children birth to three, and greater accountability.*

- *Individualized Education Plans (IEPs), offer students with documented disabilities modifications to general education standards. The process requires standardized and specialized testing, a meeting with the family to review test results, specific goals, and regular reviews.*

- *Section 504 of the Rehabilitation Act of 1973 requires schools to provide accommodations for students with documented handicaps without the same paper trail as required for IEPs. Students are entitled to the general education curriculum with accommodations generally provided within the classroom.*

- *Constitutional laws provide clarification within the school building regarding free speech, search and seizure, and due process. Other Amendments describe the requirements of general and special education. Principals must be well-versed in all laws in order to protect and serve students, staff, and families.*

Chapter 11

Resources at your Fingertips

Best Practices for Planning School Improvement Plans
Hanover Research, October 2014

Easy to follow guide on designing school improvement plans. Hanover Research followed the work of multiple districts over time to determine the most effective practices for continuous improvement in K-12 education. The essential components are identified as well as best practices and strategies. Suggestions for leadership and district level structuring were examined for effectiveness. Instruments and tools for monitoring improvement and effective models for assessment are included.

https://www.hanoverresearch.com/media/Best-Practices-for-School-Improvement-Planning.pdf

Principals Action Plan for the Every Student Succeeds Act: Providing all Students with a Well-Rounded and Complete Education.
The National Association of Elementary School Principals, February 2017

An interactive guide for designing School Improvement Plans for principals that engages district leaders as they prepare yearly ESSA requirements. Topics covered include standards and assessment; accountability; school improvement; district Title 1 plans and resources; provides professional support; student supports and academic enrichment and; high-quality early learning. Each section is divided and online making it user friendly and interactive by clicking on parts that move the users to the desired sections of the guide.

https://www.naesp.org/sites/default/files/ESSA_Action_Plan.PDF

Improving School Leadership.
Pont, Nusche, & Moorman, 2008

A guide of worldwide views of 22 educational systems by the Organization for Economic Co-Operation and Development (OECD), this guide examines policy and practices for improving education. Though written in 2008, the contributions from other countries as well as the graphs, worksheets and other guide parts are valuable to today's ever-evolving education landscape. Chapters include developing skills for effective school leadership, defining responsibilities for school improvement and change, and distributing leadership among teachers and school staff.

http://www.oecd.org/education/school/44374889.pdf

Creating a Theory of Action for Improvement in Teaching and Learning.
The University of Washington Educational Leaderships commissioned by the Wallace Foundation, 2014

A tool to create district's theory of action that leads the users step by step in an inclusive process that engages all levels of school districts from families to individual principals, superintendents and board of educations. The tool helps educators design a theory of action that "explains specific changes they intend to make to improve teaching and learning" (University of Washington, 2014).

http://info.k-12leadership.org/creating-a-theory-of-action

Transforming Student and Learning Supports: Developing a unified, comprehensive, and equitable system.
Adelman & Taylor, 2018

A common-sense guide to improving student learning by changing teacher behaviors that impact the results expected with students by using interrelated solutions. School cannot close the achievement gap without help from all stakeholders. As districts confront barriers from every angle, this book gives practical solutions to be able to design ways to mitigate those and move beyond buzzwords into action.

Quick Guide for Making School Climate Improvements.
The American Institute for Research, the National Center for Safe, Supportive Learning Environments, 2016

This guide enables schools to set into play improvements to their school climate. Defined as learning environments that support learning by having positive interpersonal relationships between staff, students and families, cutting-edge supportive practices of staff and educators, and organizational conditions, school climate is paramount to effective schools. The guide provides five activity sets to implement improvements. Areas include planning for improvements; engaging stakeholders; collecting and reporting climate data; choosing and implementing school climate interventions and; monitoring and evaluating for sustainability.

http://safesupportivelearning.ed.gov/SCIRP/Quick-Guide.
https://safesupportivelearning.ed.gov/sites/default/files/NCSSLE_SCIRP_QuickGuide508.pdf

Data Equity Walk Toolkit
Education Trust, 2018

A guide to implementing and conducting a data equity walk in your schools, with a board of education, families and students, civil rights directors, and stakeholders. The process and templates can customize by users to their individual needs.

https://west.Education Trust.org/data-equity-walk-toolkit/

NAFSCE Resources for Professionals.
The National Association for Family, School and Community Engagement

NAFSCE is a national membership organization devoted to improving partnerships between families, schools and their communities. The researchable resource library is full of articles for improvement and enhancement of partnership programs. The tools section includes toolkits for easy implementation as well as ones for evaluation. Live interactive webinars are achieved and offered throughout the year. The site includes tools to set engagement or partnership plans into motions as well as evaluation tools.

https://www.nafsce.org/general/custom.asp?page=resources

Universal Design for Learning
CAST, 2018

CAST is the home base for universal design for learning. Originally called The Center for Applied Special Technology, CAST uses creative research and strategic partnerships to find new and creative learning tools based on universal design for learning (UDL). UDL is a framework that improves learning for all students based on scientific principles.

http://www.cast.org/

Gold Standard Project Based Learning
Buck Institute for Education

Gold Standard Project Based Learning (GS-PBL) provides personalized learning solutions based on the belief that students learn more through deep and extensive project work using a framework to guide their thinking. Educators become facilitators of learning and students conclude by sharing their final projects with others.

http://www.bie.org/about/what_pbl

or

http://www.bie.org/about

Technology Standards for Education Leaders, Educators, and Students International Society for Technology in Education (ISTE), 2018

ISTE offers a full complement of tools to ensure schools are meeting the technology needs of all students. Using new standards, design tools, and frameworks, administrators, educators, students, and others are able to update and implement the most effective technology integration.

https://www.iste.org/

Technology Progression using the SAMR model

While no specific website is dedicated to the SAMR model, here is a quick video and article that both explain the differences between substitution, augmentation, modification, and redefinition.

https://www.youtube.com/watch?v=SC5ARwUkVQg and

https://www.edsurge.com/news/2018-02-01-how-samr-and-tech-can-help-teachers-truly-transform-assessment

References

A&E Network. (2018). *Brown v. board of education.* Retrieved from https://www.history.com/topics/black-history/brown-v-board-of-education-of-topeka

Accelerate Learning. (2018). *Introducing stemscopes.* Retrieved from https://stemscopes.com/

Achievement Network. (n.d.). *Interim assessments.* Retrieved from http://www.achievementnetwork.org/our-support-for-schools/

Adelman, H, & Taylor, L. (2018). Transforming Student and Learning Supports: Developing a Unified, Comprehensive, and Equitable System. Cognella Academic Publishers

Akiba, M., & LeTendre, G. (2017). *International handbook of teacher quality and policy.* New York, NY: Routledge.

Alexander, N.A. & Jang, S.T. (2017). Equity and efficiency of Minnesota educational expenditures with a focus on English learners, 2003-1022: A retrospective look in a time of accountability. *Education Policy Analysis Archives 1*(25) 16. DOI: 10.14507/epaa.25.2811

Alexander, K. & Morgan, S.L. (2016). The Colman report at 50: Its legacy and implications for future research on equal opportunity. *Russell Sage Foundation Journal of the Social Sciences, 2*(5), 1-6. DOI: 10.7758/RSF.2016.2.5.01

American Psychological Association. (2015). *Supporting transgender and gender diverse students in schools: Key recommendations for school administrators.* Retrieved from https://www.apa.org/pi/lgbt/programs/safe-supportive/lgbt/school-administrators.pdf

Baeder, J. (2018). *Now we're talking! 21 days to high-performance instructional leadership.* Bloomington, IL: Solution Tree

Bakar, Z.A., Yun, L.M., Keow, N.G., & Li, T.H. (2014). Goal-setting principles: A lesson from practitioners. *Journal of Education and Learning,* 8(1), 41-50. DOI: 10.11591/edulearn.v8i1.204

Bangs, J. & MacBeth, J. (2012). Collective leadership: the role of teacher unions in encouraging teachers to take the lead in their own learning and in teacher policy. *Professional Development in Education, 38*(2), 331-343. DOI: 10.1080/19415257.2012.657879

Baquedano-Lopez, P., Alexander, R., & Hernandez, S. (2013). Equity issues in parental and community involvement in schools: What teacher educators need to know. *Review of Research in Education, 37*(1), 149-182. DOI: 10.3102/0091732X12459718

Barile, N. (2015). 10 Tips for successful goals with students, Ed Weekly. Retrieved from https://www.edweek.org/tm/articles/2015/01/20/10-tips-for-setting-successful-goals-with.html

Barnum, M. (2018). *Do community schools and wraparound services boost academics? Here's what we know.* Retrieved from https://www.chalkbeat.org/posts/us/2018/02/20/do-community-schools-and-wraparound-services-boost-academics-heres-what-we-know/

Baron, E. J. (2018). The effect of teachers' unions on student achievement: Evidence from Wisconsin's Act 10. *SSRN Electronic Journal*, 1-44. doi:10.2139/ssrn.3001417

Baskwill, J. (2013). *Attention grabbing tools for involving parents in their children's learning.* Portland, ME: Stenhouse Publishers

Bass, B.M. & Riggio, R.E. (2014). *Transformational leadership.* New York, NY: Routledge.

Bayar, A. (2014). The components of effective professional development activities in terms of teachers' perspective. *International Online Journal of Educational Sciences*, 6 (2), 319-327. Retrieved from https://files.eric.ed.gov/fulltext/ED552871.pdf

Bendikson, L., Robinson, V., & Hattie, J. (2012). Principal instructional leadership and secondary school performance. *SET: Research information for teachers*, 1, 1-7. Retrieved from http://www.nzcer.org.nz/system/files/set2012_1_002.pdf

Benjamin, T.L. & Black, R.S. (2012). Resilience theory: Risk and protective factors for novice special education teachers. *Journal of the American Academy of Special Education Professionals.* Retrieved from https://files.eric.ed.gov/fulltext/EJ1135719.pdf

Bill & Melinda Gates Foundation. (2015). *Teachers know best: Making data work for teachers and students.* Retrieved from https://www.lexialearning.com/sites/default/files/resources/Research_External_Gates_Teachers_Know_Best_Making_Data_Work.pdf

Bisk Education. (2018). *Current issues I school law facing school administrators.* Retrieved from https://www.uscranton.com/resources/education/current-issues-in-school-law-facing-school-administrators/#.Wtp8Z4jwZPY

Blanchard, K & Broadwell, R. (2018). Servant leadership in action. Oakland, CA: Berrett-Koehler

Bodnarchuk, M. (2016). The role of principal as instructional leader. *SELU Research Review Journal*, 1(1), 5-15. Retrieved from https://selu.usask.ca/documents/research-and-publications/srrj/SRRJ-1-1-Bodnarchuk.pdf

Bogotch, I., Schoorman, D., & Reyes-Guerra, D. (2017). Educational curriculum leadership as "currere" and praxis. *Leadership and Policy in Schools*, 16(2), 303-327. DOI: 10.1080/15700763.2017.1298815

Boser, U. (2014). Teacher diversity revisited. *Center for American Progress.* Retrieved from https://www.americanprogress.org/issues/race/reports/2014/05/04/88962/teacher-diversity-revisited/

Boston, M.D., Henrick, E.C., Gibbons, L.K., Berebitsky, D. & Colby, G.T. (2017). Investigating how to support principals as instructional leaders in mathematics. *Journal of Research on Leadership Education* 12(3), 183-214. DOI: 10.1177/1942775116640254

Boudett, K.P., City, E.A., & Murnane, R.J. (2017). *Data wise: A step-by-step guide to using assessment results to improve teaching and learning* (4th ed.). Cambridge, MA: Harvard Education Press.

Bowers, A.J., Shoho, A.R., & Barnett, B.G. (2014). *Using data in schools to inform leadership and decision making*. Charlotte, NC: Information Age Publishing

Brenchley, C. (2015). *What is ESEA?* Retrieved from https://blog.ed.gov/2015/04/what-is-esea/

Brunner, E. J., & Squires, T. (2013). The bargaining power of teachers' unions and the allocation of school resources. *Journal of Urban Economics, 76*, 15-27. doi:10.1016/j.jue.2013.01.003.

Buchanan, J., Prescott, A., Schuck, S., Aubusson, P., Burke, P., & Louviere, J. (2013). Teacher retention and attrition: Views of early career teachers. *Australian Journal of Teacher Education, 38*(3), 106-121. doi:10.14221/ajte.2013v38n3.9

Buonomo, M., Fatigante, M., & Fiorilli, C. (2017). *Teachers' burnout: Risk and protective factors.* Retrieved from https://benthamopen.com/FULLTEXT/TOPSYJ-10-190

Burgess, S. & Houf, B. (2017). *Lead like a pirate: Make school amazing for your students and staff*. San Diego, CA: Dave Burgess Consulting.

Burns, J.M. (1978). *Leadership*. New York, NY: Harper Row

Buske, R., & Zlatkin-Troitschanskaia, O. (2018). Investigating principals' data use in school. *Educational Management Administration & Leadership*.

Calik, T., Sezgin, F., Kavgaci, H., & Cagatay Kilinc, A. (2012). Examination of relationships between instructional leadership of school principals and self-efficacy of teachers and collective teacher efficacy. *Educational Sciences: Theory and Practice, 12*(4), 2498-2504. Retrieved from https://eric.ed.gov/?id=EJ1002859

Carini, R.M. (2002). Teacher union and student achievement. In A. Molnar, *School Reform Proposals: The Research Evidence*, 197-216. New York, NY: Information Age Publishers

Carver-Thomas, D. (2018). *Diversifying the teaching profession: How to recruit and retain teachers of color.* Retrieved from https://learningpolicyinstitute.org/product/diversifying-teaching-profession-report

CAST. (2018a). *About universal design for learning.* Retrieved from http://www.cast.org/our-work/about-udl.html#.WwjEM4gvyuU

CAST. (2018b). *The UDL guidelines.* Retrieved from http://udlguidelines.cast.org/?utm_medium=web&utm_campaign=none&utm_source=cast-about-udl

Cauler, H.E. (2014). *Effects of technology on brain development and the institution of education.*
Retrieved from https://medium.com/@harriscauler/effects-of-technology-on-brain-development-and-the-institution-of-education-e7dc5b12c72c

Center for Educational Leadership. (2014). *Creating a theory of action.* Retrieved from http://info.k-12leadership.org/hs-fs/hub/381270/file-2166618739-

pdf/documents/webinar-presentation-pdfs/creating-a-theory-of-action.pdf

Center for Parent Information & Resources. (2017). *IDEA-the Individuals with Disabilities Act*. Retrieved from http://www.parentcenterhub.org/idea/#summaries

Center for Public Education. (2016). *Educational equity: A primer*. Retrieved from http://www.centerforpubliceducation.org/research/educational-equity-primer

Center for Social Inclusion. (2017). *Capacity Building*. Retrieved from https://www.centerforsocialinclusion.org/our-work/our-four-strategies/capacity-building/

Center on Great Teachers and Leaders at American Institutes for Research. (2017). *Principals action plan for the Every Student Succeeds Act: Providing all students with a well-rounded and complete education*. Retrieved from https://www.gtlcenter.org/sites/default/files/Principals_ActionPlan_ESSA.pdf

Common Core State Standards Initiative. (2018). *What parents should know*. Retrieved from http://www.corestandards.org/what-parents-should-know/

Concordia University-Portland. (2013). *Four instructional leadership skills principals need*. Retrieved from https://education.cu-portland.edu/blog/leaders-link/four-instructional-leadership-skills-principals-need/

Cone, K. *Short history of the 504 sit in*. Retrieved from https://dredf.org/504-sit-in-20th-anniversary/short-history-of-the-504-sit-in/

Connecticut Center for School Change. (2018). *What we do*. Retrieved from http://www.ctschoolchange.org/what-we-do/

Council for Exceptional Children. (2018). *Understanding the differences between IDEA and Section 504*. Retrieved from http://www.ldonline.org/article/6086/

Cowen, J. M., & Strunk, K. O. (2015). The impact of teachers unions on educational outcomes: What we know and what we need to learn. *Economics of Education Review, 48*, 208-223. doi:10.1016/j.econedurev.2015.02.006

Curriculum Associates. (2017). *Why i-Ready?* Retrieved from https://www.curriculumassociates.com/products/iready/iready-builtforcommoncore.aspx

Curtis, C. (2012). Why do they choose to teach-and why do they leave?: A study of middle school and high school mathematics teachers. *Academic OneFile, 132*(4), 779-788. Retrieved from https://eric.ed.gov/?id=EJ994242

D2L. (2018). *We're transforming the way the world learns*. Retrieved from https://www.d2l.com/about/

Danbury Public Schools. (2011). Theory of Action. Retrieved from http://www.danbury.k12.ct.us/UserFiles/Servers/Server_539114/File/District/Central%20Office%20Department/Deputy%20Superintendent/Theory%20of%20Action.pdf

Darden, E.C. (2006). *Search and seizure, due process, and public schools*. Retrieved from http://www.centerforpubliceducation.org/research/search-and-seizure-due-process-and-public-schools

Darling-Hammond, L., Beardsley, A., Haertel, E., & Rothstein, J. (2011). *Evaluating teacher evaluation: What we know about value-added models and other methods*. 1-18. Retrieved from http://citeseerx.ist.psu.edu/viewdoc/download?doi=10.1.1.385.1708&rep=rep1&type=pdf

Datnow, A. (2017). *Opening or closing doors for students? Equity and data-driven decision-making*. Retrieved from https://research.acer.edu.au/cgi/viewcontent.cgi?article=1317&context=research_conferenceOpening+or+closing+doors+for+students?++Equity+and+data-driven+decision-making

D'Auria, J. (2015). Learn to avoid or overcome leadership obstacles. *Kappan*, 96(5), 52-54, https://doi.org/10.1177/0031721715569471

DeMatthews, D. & Mawhinney, H. (2014). Social justice leadership and inclusion: Exploring challenges in an urban struggling to address inequities. *Educational Administration Quarterly, 50*, 844-881. DOI: 101177/0013161X13514440

Desimone, L.M., & Garet, M.S. (2015). Best practices in teacher's professional development in the United States. *Psychology, Society, & Education*, 7(3), 252-263. Retrieved from http://hub.mspnet.org/index.cfm/31536

Desimone, L.M., & Pak, K. (2017). Instructional coaching as high-quality professional development. *Theory Into Practice*, 56(1), 3-12. DOI: 10.1080/00405841.2016.1241947

DiCarlo, M. (2011). *Revisiting the effect of teachers unions on student test scores*. Retrieved from http://www.shankerinstitute.org/blog/revisiting-effect-teachers-unions-student-test-scores

Discovery Education. (2018). *Free student resources*. Retrieved from http://www.discoveryeducation.com/students/?campaign=flyout_students

Doney, P. A. (2013). Fostering resilience: A necessary skill for teacher retention. *Journal of Science Teacher Education, 24*(4), 645-664. doi:10.1007/s10972-012-9324-x

Donnella, L. (2016). *When these Latinos tell immigration stories, they push beyond fairy tales*. Retrieved from https://www.npr.org/sections/codeswitch/2016/10/20/497931475/when-these-latinos-tell-immigration-stories-they-push-beyond-fairy-tales

Dreambox Learning. (2018). *Administrator*. Retrieved from http://www.dreambox.com/

DuFour, R., DuFour, R., Eaker, R., & Mattos, T.W. (2016). *Learning by Doing: A handbook for professional learning communities at work* (3rd ed.). Bloomington, IL: Solution Tree

DuFour, R. & Mattos, M. (2013). *How do principals improve schools?* Retrieved from https://www.cisdctl.com/uploads/1/3/3/4/133401/st-dufour-mattos-article.pdf

Duncan, A. (2014). *Department of Education release of new family engagement framework*. Retrieved from https://www.youtube.com/watch?v=BR2e0HVKa4U

Earl, L., & Katz, S. (2002). Leading Schools in a Data-Rich World. *Second International Handbook of Educational Leadership and Administration,* 1003-1022. doi:10.1007/978-94-010-0375-9_34

Education Trust. (n.d.). *The school improvement process.* Retrieved from: https://Education Trust.org/students-cant-wait/school-improvement-process/

Edutopia. (2015). *Gaining understanding on what your students know.* Retrieved from https://www.edutopia.org/practice/exit-tickets-checking-understanding

Edutopia. (2018). *The big list of educational grants and resources.* Retrieved from https://www.edutopia.org/grants-and-resources

Egalite, A. J. Fusarelli, B.C., & Fusarelli, L. D. (2017). Will decentralization affect educational inequity? The Every Student Succeeds Act. *Educational Administration Quarterly, 53*(1). DOI: 10.1177/0013161X17735869

Epstein, J.L. (2018). *School, family, and community partnerships* (2nd ed.). New York, NY: Routledge.

Fagan, D. (2018). *Teachers' union shows true colors.* Retrieved from http://www.theadvocate.com/baton_rouge/opinion/article_8fb4e016-47e3-11e8-8738-07740dc4a6f0.html

Feiman-Nemser, S. (2012). Beyond solo teaching. *Educational Leadership, 69*(8), 10-16. Retrieved from http://pi-34.pbworks.com/w/file/fetch/56517303/Beyond%20Solo%20Teaching.pdf

Fenton, B. (n.d.). *New leaders for new schools: Forming aligned instructional leadership teams.* Retrieved from http://www.ascd.org/ascd-express/vol5/504-fenton.aspx

Ferlazzo, L. (2011). Involvement or engagement? *Education Leadership, 68*(8), 10-14. Retrieved from https://eric.ed.gov/?id=EJ932180

Ferlazzo, L. (2013). The differences between parent involvement and parent engagement. *Library Media Connection, 28.*

Fink, J. (2018). *Power of the principal in schools: How to devote more time and energy to instructional leadership.* Retrieved from https://www.districtadministration.com/article/power-principal-schools

Fiorvanti, C.M.L. (2015). *Family-school communication notebooks: An effective tool for promoting learning in young children with special needs.* DOI: 10.7916/D8F76BBC

Fowler, C. S., & Walter, S. (2003). Instructional leadership: New responsibilities for a new reality. *College and Research Libraries, 64*(7), 465-468.

Frey, W.H. (2016). *Diversity defines the millennial generation.* Retrieved from https://www.brookings.edu/blog/the-avenue/2016/06/28/diversity-defines-the-millennial-generation/

Gillanders. C., McKinney, M., & Ritchie, S. (2012). What kind of school would you like for your children? Exploring minority mothers' beliefs to promote home-school partnerships. *Early Childhood Education, 40,* 285-294. Doi:10.1007/s10643-012-0514-0

Glickman, C.D., Gordon, S.P, Ross-Gordon, J.M. (2018). *Supervision and instructional leadership: A developmental approach* (10th ed.). New York, NY: Pearson.

Grant, K.B. & Ray, J.A. (2016). *Home, school, and community collaboration* (3rd ed.). Thousand Oaks, CA: SAGE

Gray, J., Kruse, S., & Tarter, J. (2016). Enabling school structures, collegial trust and academic emphasis: Antecedents of professional learning communities. *Educational Management Administration & Leadership.* DOI: 10.1177/174113215574505

Greenleaf Center for Servant Leadership. (2016). *What is servant leadership?* Retrieved from https://www.greenleaf.org/what-is-servant-leadership/

Grissom, J. A., Loeb, S., & Master, B. (2013). Effective instructional time use for school leaders. *Educational Researcher, 42*(8), 433-444. doi:10.3102/0013189x13510020

Grundler, M. & Grundler, L. (2017). *The purposeful principals: Leadership with heart.* Retrieved from https://educationcloset.com/2017/12/01/the-purposeful-principals-leadership/

Gumus, S., & Akcaoglu, M. (2013). Instructional leadership in Turkish primary schools. *Educational Management Administration & Leadership, 41*(3), 289-302. doi:10.1177/1741143212474801

Hale, E. L., & Moorman, H. M. (2003). Preparing School Principals: A National Perspective on Policy and Program Innovations. *Institute for Educational Leadership,* 1-28.

Hall, P. & Simeral, A. (2017). *Creating a culture of reflective practice: Capacity building for schoolwide success.* Alexandria, VA: ASCD

Hallinger, P. (2010). Leading educational change: Reflections on the practice of instructional and transformational leadership. *Cambridge Journal of Education, 33*(3), 329-352. doi:10.1080/0305764032000122005

Hallinger, P., & Lee, M. (2013). Mapping instructional leadership in Thailand. *Educational Management Administration & Leadership, 42*(1), 6-29. doi:10.1177/1741143213502196

Halverson, R. (2010). School Formative Feedback Systems. *Peabody Journal of Education, 85*(2), 130-146. doi:10.1080/01619561003685270

Halverson, R., & Clifford, M. (2013). Distributed instructional leadership in high schools. *Journal of School Leadership, 23*(2), 389-419.

Halverson, R., Grigg, J., Prichett, R., & Thomas, C. (2007). The new instructional leadership: Creating data-driven instructional systems in school. *Journal of School Leadership, 17*(2), 159-194.

Hamilton, L. S., Halverson, R., Jackson, S. S., Mandinach, E., Supovitz, J. A., Wayman, J., . . . Steele, J. L. (2009). *Using Student Achievement Data to Support Instructional Decision-making.* U.S. Dept. of Education, Institute of Education Sciences, National Center for Education Evaluation and Regional Assistance.

Han, Y.C., (2012). From Survivor to leaders: Stages of immigrant family involvement. *Innovative Voices in Education: Engaging Diverse Communities*. Retrieved from www.innovativevoicesineducation.com

Haneda, M., Teemant, A., & Sherman, B. (2017). Instructional coaching through dialogic interaction: helping a teacher to become agentive in her practice. *Language and Education 31*(1), 46-64. DOI: 10.1080/09500782.2016.1230127

Hanover Research. (2014). *Best practices for school improvement planning*. Retrieved from https://www.hanoverresearch.com/media/Best-Practices-for-School-Improvement-Planning.pdf

Hanover Research. (2016). *Best practice in engaging diverse families*. Retrieved from http://www.pthvp.org/wp-content/uploads/2016/10/Engaging-Diverse-Families.pdf

Hansen, M, Levesque, E.M., Quintero, D., & Valant, J. (2018). *Have we made progress on achievement gaps? Looking at evidence from the new NAEP results*. Retrieved from https://www.brookings.edu/blog/brown-center-chalkboard/2018/04/17/have-we-made-progress-on-achievement-gaps-looking-at-evidence-from-the-new-naep-results/

Harris, A., Day, C., Hopkins, D., Hadfield, M., Hargreaves, A., & Chapman, C. (2013). *Effective leadership for school improvement*. London: Routledge Falmer.

Hazell, W. (2017). *Nearly half of young teachers planning to quit over high workload*. Retrieved from https://www.tes.com/news/nearly-half-young-teachers-planning-quit-over-high-workload

Henderson, A. (2016). *Quick brief on family engagement in Every Student Succeeds Act [ESSA] of 2015*. Retrieved from https://ra.nea.org/wp-content/uploads/2016/06/FCE-in-ESSA-in-Brief.pdf

Henderson, A. T., & Berla, N. (1994). A new generation of evidence: The family is critical to student achievement. Washington, DC: National Committee for Citizens in Education.

Henderson, A.T., Mapp, K.L., Johnson, V.R., & Davies, D. (2007). *Beyond the bake sale: The essential guide to family-school partnerships*. New York, NY: The New Press.

Hendricks, M. D. (2014). Does it pay to pay teachers more?: Evidence from Texas. *SSRN Electronic Journal, 109*, 50-63. doi:10.2139/ssrn.2252576

Hernandez-Prados, A., Garcia-Sanz, P., Parra, J., & Gomariz, A. (2017). Involvement of immigrant families in the school life. *Procedia: Social and Behavioral Sciences, (237)* 157-163. DOI: 10.1016/j.sbspro.2017.02.057

Hirano, K.A. & Rowe, D.A. (2015). A conceptual model for parent involvement in secondary special education. *Journal of Disability Policy Studies, 27*(1), 43-53. DOI: 10.1177/1044207315583901

Hoerr, T.R. (2005). *The art of school leadership*. Alexandria, VA: ASCD

Hollingworth, L., Olsen, D., Asikin-Garmager, A., & Winn, K.M. (2017). Initiating conversations and opening doors: How principals establish a positive building culture to sustain school improvement efforts. *Educational Management Administration & Leadership*. DOI: 10.1177/1741143217720461

References

Hood, K. (2014). *Why use social media to reach parents in your district?* Retrieved from
httsp://nspra.org/communicationmatters/oct2014/khood

Horng, E., & Loeb, S. (2010). New thinking about instructional leadership. *Phi Delta Kappan, 92*(3), 66-69. doi:10.1177/003172171009200319

Horowitz, S.H., Rawe, J., & Wittaker, M.C. (2017). The state of learning disabilities: Understanding the 1 in 5: Executive summary. *National Center for Learning Disabilities.* Retrieved from https://www.ncld.org/executive-summary

Huber, S.G. & Skedsmo, G. (2016). Teacher evaluation – accountability and improving teacher practices. *Educational Assessment, Evaluation, and Accountability.* DOI: 10.1007/s11092-016-9241-1

Hughes, G. D. (2012). Teacher retention: Teacher characteristics, school characteristics, organizational characteristics, and teacher efficacy. *The Journal of Educational Research, 105*(4), 245-255. doi:10.1080/00220671.2011.584922

Hutt, M. (2017). *Benefits of interactive whiteboards in the classroom.* Retrieved from https://www.eztalks.com/whiteboard/benefits-of-interactive-whiteboards-in-the-classroom.html

IDEA. (n.d.). *IDEA regulations technical changes.* Retrieved from https://sites.ed.gov/idea/idea-regulations-technical-changes/

Ikemoto, G. S., & Marsh, J. A. (2007). Cutting Through the "Data-Driven" Mantra: Different Conceptions of Data-Driven Decision-making. *Evidence and Decision-making, 106*(1), 105-131.

Illinois Federation of Teachers. (2018). *AFT professional development.* Retrieved from
https://www.ift-aft.org/professional-development/aft-professional-development

Ingersoll, R., Merrill, L., & May, H. (2012). Retaining teachers: How preparation matters. *Educational Leadership, 69*(8), 30-34. Retrieved from https://eric.ed.gov/?id=EJ988729

IXL Learning. (2018). *At IXL learning...* Retrieved from https://www.ixl.com/company/

Izadinia, M. (2015). A closer look at the role of mentor teachers in shaping preservice teachers' professional identity. *Teaching and Teacher Education, 52,* 1-10. doi:10.1016/j.tate.2015.08.003

Jacobson, L., Rollins, R. S., Brown, J., & Naviasky, H. (2016). Patterns of practice: Case studies of early childhood education & family engagement in community schools. *Institute for Educational Leadership.* Retrieved from https://eric.ed.gov/?id=ED570656

Jensen, E. (2013). *Engaging students with poverty in mind: Practical strategies for raising student achievement.* Alexandria, VA: ASCD

Jensen, B., Downing, P., & Clark, A. (2017). Preparing to lead: Lessons in principal development from high performing education systems. *Center on International Education Benchmarking.* Retrieved from http://ncee.org/wp-content/uploads/2017/10/PreparingtoLeadFINAL101817.pdf

Jiang, J. Y., Sporte, S. E., & Luppescu, S. (2015). Teacher perspectives on evaluation reform. *Educational Researcher, 44*(2), 105-116. doi:10.3102/0013189x15575517

Johnson, S. M., Kraft, M. A., & Papay, J. P. (2011). How context matters in high-need schools: The effects of teachers' working conditions on their professional satisfaction and their students' achievement. *Project on the Next Generation of Teachers Harvard Graduate School of Education,* 1-57. Retrieved from https://scholar.harvard.edu/files/mkraft/files/johnson_kraft_papay_teacher_working_conditions_final.pdf

Kazakoff, E. & Mitchell, A. (2017). *Cultivating a growth mindset with educational technology.* Retrieved from https://www.lexialearning.com/sites/default/files/resources/Cultivating-Growth-Mindset-with-Educational-Technology-White-Paper.pdf

Kegan, R. & Lahey, L.L. (2009). *Immunity to Change: How to Overcome It and Unlock the Potential in Yourself and Your Organization.* Cambridge, MA: Harvard Business Press

Kegan, R. & Lahey, L.L. (2016). *An everyone culture: Becoming a deliberately developmental organization.* Boston, MA: Harvard Business Review Press

Killion, J. (2012). Meet the promise of content standards: The principal. *Leaning Forward.* Retrieved from https://learningforward.org/docs/commoncore/meetpromiseprincipal.pdf

Klein, A. (2016). *The Every Student Succeeds Act: An ESSA overview.* Retrieved from https://www.edweek.org/ew/issues/every-student-succeeds-act/index.html

Klein, A. (2018). *ESSA progress report: How the new law is moving from policy to practice.* Retrieved from https://www.edweek.org/ew/articles/2018/04/04/essa-progress-report-how-the-new-law.html

Klein, R. (2015). *In 10 years, America's classrooms are going to be much more diverse than they are now.* Retrieved from http://www.nccp.org/publications/pub_1194.html

Knowles, M. (1984). *Andragogy in Action.* San Francisco: Jossey-Bass.

Koball, H. & Jaing, Y. (2018). *Basic facts about low-income children: Children under 18 years, 2016.* Retrieved from http://www.nccp.org/publications/pub_1194.html

Koedel, C., Mihaly, K., & Rockoff, J.E. (2015). *Value-Added modeling: A review.* Retrieved from https://economics.missouri.edu/working-papers/2015/wp1501_koedel.pdf

Kosciw, J.G., Grgeytak, E.A., Bartkiewicz, M.J., Boesen, M.J., & Palmer, N.A. (2012). *The 2011 national school climate survey: The experiences of lesbian, gay, bisexual and transgender youth in our nation's schools.* Retrieved from https://www.glsen.org/sites/default/files/2011%20National%20School%20Climate%20Survey%20Full%20Report.pdf

Kostelkin, M.J. & Grady, M.L. (2009). *Getting it right from the start: The principal's guide to early childhood education.* Thousand Oaks, CA: Corwin

Koyama, J. (2013). Principals as Bricoleurs. *Educational Administration Quarterly, 50*(2), 279-304. doi:10.1177/0013161x13492796

Larmer, J., Mergendoller, J., & Boss, S. (2015). *Setting the standard for project based learning: A proven approach to rigorous classroom instruction.* Alexandria, VA: ASCD.

Lee, A.M. (2018). *Individuals with Disabilities Act (IDEA): What you need to know.* Retrieved from https://www.understood.org/en/school-learning/your-childs-rights/basics-about-childs-rights/individuals-with-disabilities-education-act-idea-what-you-need-to-know

Lee, C. (2017). *What is interactive whiteboard.* Retrieved from https://www.eztalks.com/whiteboard/what-is-interactive-whiteboard.html

Lee, M., Hallinger, P., & Walker, A. (2012). A distributed perspective on instructional leadership in international baccalaureate (IB) schools. *Educational Administration Quarterly, 48*(4), 664-698. doi:10.1177/0013161x11436271

Leef, G. (2018). *Janus v. AFSCME: Perhaps this time the court will take the first amendment seriously.* Retrieved from https://www.forbes.com/sites/georgeleef/2018/03/02/janus-v-afscme-perhaps-this-time-the-court-will-take-the-first-amendment-seriously/#c284eef57918

Le Fevre, D. M., & Robinson, V. M. (2014). The interpersonal challenges of instructional leadership. *Educational Administration Quarterly, 51*(1), 58-95. doi:10.1177/0013161x13518218

Legeros, L. (2016). *Facilitating community conversations about education: 4 lessons learned.* Retrieved from http://tiie.w3.uvm.edu/blog/facilitating-community-conversations-education/#.WzT4CtJKg2w

Leithwood, K. (2010). Characteristics of school districts that are exceptionally effective in closing the achievement gap. *Leadership & Policy in Schools, 9*(3), 245-291.

Lendrum, A., Barlow, A., & Humphries, A. (2013). Developing positive school-home relationships through structured conversation with parents of special needs and disabilities. *Journal of Research in Special Needs Education, 15*(2), 87-96. DOI: 10.1111/1471-3802.12023

Lexia Learning. (2018). *RTI and MTSS: Do you know the difference between these support systems?* Retrieved from https://www.lexialearning.com/blog/rti-and-mtss-do-you-know-difference-between-these-support-systems

Liptak, A. (2018). *Supreme court ruling delivers a sharp blow to labor unions.* Retrieved from https://www.nytimes.com/2018/06/27/us/politics/supreme-court-unions-organized-labor.html

Locke, E.A. & Latham, G.P. (1990). *A theory of goal setting & task performance.* New York, NY: Pearson.

Loeb, S., Kalogrides, D., & Beteille, T. (2012). Effective schools: teacher hiring, assignment, development, and retention. *Education Finance and Policy, 7*(3), 269-304. doi:10.3386/w17177

Longley, R. (2017). *School prayer: Separation of church and state: Why Johnny can't pray – at school.* Retrieved from https://www.thoughtco.com/separation-of-church-and-state-3572154

Lott, J., & Kenny, L. W. (2013). State teacher union strength and student achievement. *Economics of Education Review, 35,* 93-103. doi:10.1016/j.econedurev.2013.03.006.

Loughran, J. (2014). Professionally developing as a teacher educator. *Journal of teacher education,* 65(4), 271-283. DOI: 10.1177/0022487114533386

Louis, K. S., & Robinson, V. M. (2012). External mandates and instructional leadership: School leaders as mediating agents. *Journal of Educational Administration, 50*(5), 629-665. doi:10.1108/09578231211249853

Louis, K.S. & Murphy, J. (2017). Trust, caring and organizational learning: the leader's role. *Journal of Educational Administration, 55*(1) 103-126. DOI: 10.1108/JEA-07-2016-0077

Loveless, T. (2016). *The 2016 Brown Center report on American education: How well are American students learning?* Washington, DC: The Brookings Institution. Retrieved from   https://www.brookings.edu/wp-content/uploads/2016/03/Brown-Center-Report-2016.pdf

Lunenburg, F. C. (2010). The Principal and the School: What Do Principals Do? *National Forum of Educational and Supervision Journal, 27*(4), 1-13. Retrieved from
http://www.nationalforum.com/Electronic%20Journal%20Volumes/Lunenburg,%20Fred%20C.%20The%20Principal%20and%20the%20School%20-%20What%20Do%20Principals%20Do%20NFEASJ%20V27,%20N4,%202010.pdf

Luo, M. (2008). Structural Equation Modeling for High School Principals' Data-Driven Decision-making: An Analysis of Information Use Environments. *Educational Administration Quarterly, 44*(5), 603-634. doi:10.1177/0013161x08321506

Lynch, M. (2012). Recruiting, retaining, and fairly compensating our teachers. *International Journal of Progressive Education, 8*(2), 121-135. Retrieved from http://dergipark.gov.tr/download/article-file/237189

Maciag, M. (2016). *The states that spend the most (and least) on education.* Retrieved from
http://www.governing.com/topics/education/gov-education-funding-states.html

Mader, J. (2012). *The rise of teacher unions: A look at union impact over the years.* Retrieved from http://hechingered.org/content/the-rise-of-teacher-unions-a-look-at-union-impact-over-the-years_5601/

Manzo, J. (2016). *Teachers unions are associated with higher test scores.* Retrieved from https://illinoisupdate.com/2016/04/19/teachers-unions-are-associated-with-higher-student-test-scores/

Mapp, K. (2010). Taking leadership, innovating change: Profiles in family, school, and community engagement. *National Family, School, and Community Engagement Working Group.* Harvard Family Research Project. 1-17.

Mapp, K.L., Carver, I, & Lander, J. (2017). *Powerful partnerships: A teacher's guide to engaging families for student success.* New York, NY: Scholastic

Mapp, K.L. & Kuttner, P. (2014). *Partners in education: A dual-capacity framework for family-school partnerships.* Austin, TX: Southwest Educational Development Laboratory

Marsh, J. A., Bertrand, M., & Huguet, A. (2015). Using Data to Alter Instructional Practice: The Mediating Role of Coaches and Professional Learning Communities. *Teachers College Record, 117*(4), 1-40.

Marsh, J. A., & Farrell, C. C. (2014). How leaders can support teachers with data-driven decision-making. *Educational Management Administration & Leadership, 43*(2), 269-289. doi:10.1177/1741143214537229

Marsh, J. A., McCombs, J. S., & Martorell, F. (2009). How Instructional Coaches Support Data-Driven Decision-making. *Educational Policy, 24*(6), 872-907. doi:10.1177/0895904809341467

Marsh, J. A., Pane, J. F., & Hamilton, L. S. (2006). *Making sense of data-driven decision-making in education: Evidence from recent RAND research.* Santa Monica, CA: RAND.

Marzano, R. J. (2012). The two purposes of teacher evaluation. *Educational Leadership*, 14-19. Retrieved from https://www.scribd.com/document/347638116/the-two-purposes-of-teacher-evaluation-by-robert-marzano

Marzano, R.J., Warrick, P.B., Rains, C.L., & DuFour, R. (2018). *Leading a high reliability school.* Bloomington, IL: Solution Tree

Marzano, R.J. & Waters, T. (2009). *District leadership that works: Striking the right balance.* Bloomington, IL: Solution Tree.

Massachusetts Department of Elementary and Secondary Education. (2012). Massachusetts model system for educator evaluation. *Educator Evaluation*, 1-17. Retrieved from http://www.doe.mass.edu/edeval/model/

Massachusetts Department of Elementary and Secondary Education. (n.d.). *Guidance for Massachusetts public schools: Creating a safe and supportive school environment: Nondiscrimination on the basis of gender identity.* Retrieved from http://www.doe.mass.edu/sfs/lgbtq/handouts/D-GenderIdentity.pdf

Mathewson, T.G. (2016). *Schools are under federal pressure to translate for immigrant parents.* Retrieved from http://hechingerreport.org/schools-federal-pressure-translate-immigrant-families/

McKenna, M.K. and Millen, J. (2013). Look! Listen! Learn! Parent narratives and grounded theory models of parent voice, presence, and engagement in K-12 education. *School Community Journal*, v23 n1 p9-48 2013. Retrieved from https://eric.ed.gov/?id=EJ1004331

McLeskey, J. and Waldon, N. L. (2015). Effective leadership makes schools truly inclusive. *Kappan, 96*(5), 69-73. https://doi.org/10.1177/0031721715569474

McKnight, K., Venkateswaran, N., Laird, J., Robles, J., & Shalev, T. (2017). *Mindful shifts and parent teacher home visits.* Retrieved from http://www.pthvp.org/wp-content/uploads/2018/02/PTHV_Study1_Report.pdf

Mead, A. E. (2017). *Understanding parent's school experiences and how it influences their intent to engage with their child's school* (Unpublished doctoral dissertation). Northeastern University, Boston, MA.

Meador, D. (2017). *Pros and cons of joining a teacher's union.* Retrieved from https://www.thoughtco.com/weighing-the-decision-to-join-a-teachers-union-3194787

Mense, E. G., & Crain-Dorough, M. (2018). *Data leadership for K-12 schools in a time of accountability.* Hershey, PA: IGI Global, Information Science Reference

Meristo, M., & Eisenschmidt, E. (2014). Novice teachers' perceptions of school climate and self-efficacy. *International Journal of Educational Research, 67,* 1-10. doi:10.1016/j.ijer.2014.04.003

Microsoft. (2018). *Office Resources for education.* Retrieved from https://products.office.com/en-us/student/office-in-education

Miller, S. (2017). *Five models of technology transition to bridge the gap between digital natives and digital immigrants.* Retrieved from https://insights.sei.cmu.edu/sei_blog/2017/11/five-models-of-technology-transition-to-bridge-the-gap-between-digital-natives-and-digital-immigrant.html

Miller, K., Dillworth-Bart, J., & Hane, A. (2011). Maternal recollections of schooling and children's school preparation. *The Community Journal, 21*(2), 161-184.

Mirel, J. & Goldin, S. (2012). *Alone in the classroom: Why teachers are too isolated.* Retrieved from https://www.theatlantic.com/national/archive/2012/04/alone-in-the-classroom-why-teachers-are-too-isolated/255976/

Mitchell, C. (2016). *Home-school connections help ELLs and their parents.* Retrieved from https://www.edweek.org/ew/articles/2016/05/11/home-school-connections-help-ells-and-their-parents.html

Murray, J. (2014). Critical issues facing school leaders concerning data-informed decision-making. *School Leadership & Management, 33*(2), 169-177. doi:10.1080/13632434.2013.773882

Murray, M. (2017). *Total quality management (TQM) and quality improvement.* Retrieved from https://www.thebalance.com/total-quality-management-tqm-2221200

Mystery Science. (2018). *Our mission.* Retrieved from https://mysteryscience.com/mission

National Association for Family, School, and Community Engagement. (2016). *Family engagement toolkits.* Retrieved from https://www.nafsce.org/page/Toolkits?

National Association of Elementary School Principals. (2017). *Principals Action Plan for the Every Student Succeeds Act: Providing all students with a well-rounded and complete education.* Retrieved from https://www.gtlcenter.org/sites/default/files/Principals_ActionPlan_ESSA.pdf

National Association of Secondary School Principals and National Association of Elementary School Principals. (2013). *Leadership matters: What the re-*

References

search says about the importance of principal leadership. Retrieved from http://www.naesp.org/sites/default/files/LeadershipMatters.pdf

National Center for Education Statistics. (2014). *Enrollment and percentage distribution of enrollment in public elementary and secondary schools, by race/ethnicity and level of education: Fall 1998 through fall 2023*. Retrieved from https://nces.ed.gov/programs/digest/d13/tables/dt13_203.60.asp?current=yes

National Low Income Housing Coalition. (2014). *40 years ago: The Rehabilitation Act of 1973 passed*. Retrieved from http://nlihc.org/article/40-years-ago-rehabilitation-act-1973-passed

National Science Teachers Association. (2014). *About the next generation science standards*. Retrieved from http://ngss.nsta.org/About.aspx

NCAC Staff. (2013). *The First Amendment in schools: A resource guide*. Retrieved from http://ncac.org/resource/first-amendment-in-schools

Neumerski, C. M. (2012). Rethinking instructional leadership, a review. *Educational Administration Quarterly, 49*(2), 310-347. doi:10.1177/0013161x12456700

Nunez, S. (2017). *Engaging ELL families: 20 strategies for school leaders*. Retrieved from http://www.adlit.org/article/42781/

Oberman, M.E. & Boudett, K.P. (2015). Eight steps to becoming data wise. *Educational Leadership 73*(3). Retrieved from http://www.ascd.org/publications/educational-leadership/nov15/vol73/num03/Eight-Steps-to-Becoming-Data-Wise.aspx

O'Donnell, J., & Kirkner, S. L. (2014). The impact of a collaborative family involvement program: Latino families and children's educational preferences. *School and Community Journal, 24*(1), 211-234.

Ostovar-Nameghi, S.A. & Sheikhahmadi, M. (2016). *From teacher isolation to teacher collaboration: Theoretical perspectives and empirical findings. 9*(5) 197. DOI: 10.5539/let.v9n5p197

Park, V., & Datnow, A. (2009). Co-constructing distributed leadership: District and school connections in data-driven decision-making. *School Leadership & Management, 29*(5), 477-494. doi:10.1080/13632430903162541

Parker, D.C. (2017). The impact of professional development on poverty, schooling, and literacy practices: Teacher narratives and reformation of mindset. *Cogent Education, 4*(1). DOI: 10.1080/2331186C.2017.1279381

Parr, M., Vander-Dussen, M. (2017). Family-School (Dis)Engagement: Understanding what it is, what it is not and what to do. *Language and Literacy, 19*(1), 48-62. DOI: 10.20360/G26G6F

Partee, G. L. (2014). Retaining teachers of color in our public schools: A critical need for action. *Center for American Progress*, 1-26. Retrieved from https://files.eric.ed.gov/fulltext/ED561078.pdf

Petty, T. M., Fitchett, P., & O'Connor, K. (2012). Attracting and keeping teachers in high-need schools. *American Secondary Education, 40*(2), 67-88. Retrieved from http://www.jstor.org/stable/43694131?seq=1#page_scan_tab_contents

Pianta, R, Hamre, B., Downer, J., Burchinal, M., Williford, A., LoCasale-Crouch, J., Howes, C., & Scott-Little, C. (2017). Early childhood professional development: Coaching and coursework effects on indicators of children's school readiness. *Early Education and Development.* DIO: 10.1080/10409289.2017.1319783

PowerSchool. (2017). *The award-winning unified classroom.* Retrieved from https://www.powerschool.com/

Prytula, M., Noonan, B., & Hellsten, L. (2013). Toward instructional leadership: Principals' perceptions of large-scale assessment in schools. *Canadian Journal of Educational Administration and Policy, 140,* 1-30. Retrieved from https://eric.ed.gov/?id=EJ1008727

Rasmussen, A. (2016). *Starting with why.* Retrieved from https://threeteacherstalk.com/2016/01/06/starting-with-why/

Raty, H. (2011). Past in the present: the way parents remember their own school years relates to the way they participate in their child's schooling and remember his/her school years. *Social Psychology of Education, 14, 347-360.*

Ravani, G. (2014). Why public education needs teachers unions. *EdSource,* 1-19. Retrieved from ttps://edsource.org/2014/why-public-education-needs-teachers-unions/65723

Ravitch, D. (n.d.). *Why teacher unions are good for teachers-and the public.* Retrieved from https://www.aft.org/periodical/american-educator/winter-2006-2007/why-teacher-unions-are-good-teachers-and

Redford, K. (2017). *Cultural competency is not a 'soft' skills.* Retrieved from https://www.edweek.org/tm/articles/2017/07/11/cultural-competency-is-not-a-soft-skill.html

Reedy, K. (2014). *9 best teaching practices for cultural competency.* Retrieved from http://www.couragerenewal.org/9-best-teaching-practices-for-cultural-competency/

Reinhorn, S. K., Johnson, S. M., & Simon, N. S. (2017). Investing in development: Six high-performing, high-poverty schools implement the Massachusetts Teacher Evaluation Policy. *Educational Evaluation and Policy Analysis, 39*(3), 383-406. doi:10.3102/0162373717690605

Rigby, J. G. (2013). Three logics of instructional leadership. *Educational Administration Quarterly, 50*(4), 610-644. doi:10.1177/0013161x13509379

Riggio, R.E. (2017). *Are teachers getting bullied?* Retrieved from https://www.psychologytoday.com/us/blog/cutting-edge-leadership/201711/are-teachers-getting-bullied

Ronfeldt, M. (2012). Where should student teachers learn to teach? *Educational Evaluation and Policy Analysis, 34*(1), 3-26. doi:10.3102/0162373711420865

RTI Network. (n.d.). *What is RTI?* Retrieved from http://www.rtinetwork.org/learn/what/whatisrti

Rubinstein, S. A., & McCarthy, J. E. (2014). Teachers unions and management partnerships: How working together improves student achievement. *Center for American Progress,* 1-28. Retrieved from https://eric.ed.gov/?id=ED561086

Samuels, C.A. (2016). *Number of U.S. students in special education ticks upwards*. Retrieved from https://www.edweek.org/ew/articles/2016/04/20/number-of-us-students-in-special-education.html

Sargent, M. (n.d.). *Stop and listen to immigrants' stories*. Retrieved from http://legis.wisconsin.gov/assembly/48/sargent/news/op-eds/stop-and-listen-to-immigrants-stories/

Schaefer, L., Long, J. S., & Clandinin, D. J. (2012). Questioning the research on early career teacher attrition and retention. *Alberta Journal of Educational Research, 58*(1), 106-121. Retrieved from https://eric.ed.gov/?id=EJ972425

Siemens, G., & Baker, R. S. (2012). Learning analytics and educational data mining. *Proceedings of the 2nd International Conference on Learning Analytics and Knowledge - LAK '12*, 1-3. doi:10.1145/2330601.2330661

Simmons, W. (2014). *How relevant is Brown v. Board of Education Today?* Retrieved from http://www.wbur.org/cognoscenti/2014/05/19/how-relevant-is-brown-v-board-of-education-today

Sinek, S. (2011). *Start with why: How great leaders inspire everyone to take action*. New York, NY: Penguin

Sinek, S., Mead, D., & Docker, P. (2017). *Find your why: A practical guide for discovering purpose for you and your team*. New York, NY: Penguin

Singer, A. (2013). *Rebuilding and redefining the teachers' union*. Retrieved from https://www.huffingtonpost.com/alan-singer/teachers-unions_b_4132918.html

Smith, W. C. (2015). Framing the debate over teacher unions. *Mid-Atlantic Education Review, 1*(1), 17-26. Retrieved from http://www.maereview.org/index.php/maer/article/view/5

Social Welfare History Project (2016). Elementary and Secondary Education Act of 1965. *Social Welfare History Project*. Retrieved from https://socialwelfare.library.vcu.edu/programs/education/elementary-and-secondary-education-act-of-1965/

Sofo, F., Fitzgerald, R., & Jawas, U. (2012). Instructional leadership in Indonesian school reform: Overcoming the problems to move forward. *School Leadership & Management, 32*(5), 503-522. doi:10.1080/13632434.2012.723616

Southwestern Educational Development Laboratory. (2013). Partners in education: Dual capacity-building framework for family-school partnerships. Retrieved from http://www.sedl.org/pubs/framework/

Spangler, D., Brown, S. Simmons, T., McGarvey, B., Cushenberry, D. ... Dawson, L.C. (2016). *Seizing the moment: Realizing the promise of student-centered learning*. Retrieved from http://www.wbur.org/cognoscenti/2014/05/19/how-relevant-is-brown-v-board-of-education-today

Sparks, S.D. (2016). *50 years seeking educational equality: Revisiting the Coleman report*. Retrieved from https://www.edweek.org/ew/section/multimedia/50-years-seeking-educational-equality-the-coleman-report.html

Sparks, S. D. (2018). A primer on continuous school improvement. *Education Week*, Retrieved *from www.edweek.org/ew/artilces/2018/02/07*

Stahl, G., Sharplin, E., & Kehrwald, B. (2016). Developing pre-service teachers' confidence: real-time coaching in teacher education. *International and Multidisciplinary Perspectives 17*(6), 724-738. DOI: 10.1080/14623943.2016.1206882

Steinberg, M. P., & Sartain, L. (2015). Does teacher evaluation improve school performance? Experimental evidence from Chicago's excellence in teaching project. *Education Finance and Policy, 10*(4), 535-572. doi:10.1162/edfp_a_00173

Strauss, V. (2016). The real problem isn't teachers. *Washington Post.* Retrieved from https://www.washingtonpost.com/news/answer-sheet/wp/2016/06/30/the-real-problem-isnt-teachers/?noredirect=on&utm_term=.1d8c13094d29

Stribbell, H. (2014). *Engaging your school community through social media.* Retrieved from https://www.edutopia.org/blog/engaging-school-community-social-media-howard-stribbell

Stricker, J. (2017). *3 keys to building strong instructional leadership teams.* Retrieved from http://www.insighteducationgroup.com/blog/3-keys-to-building-strong-instructional-leadership-teams

StriveTogether. (2018). *About us.* Retrieved from https://www.strivetogether.org/about/

Strunk, K. (2011). Are teachers' unions really to blame?: Collective bargaining agreements and their relationships with district resource allocation and student performance in California. *Education Finance and Policy,* 6(3), 354–398. doi:10.1162/edfp_a_00039

Strunk, K., & McEachin, A. (2011). Accountability under constraint. *American Educational Research Journal, 48*(4), 871–903. doi:10.3102/0002831211401006

Sun, J., Johnson, B., & Przybylski, R. (2016). Leading with data: An increasingly important feature of school leadership. *International Studies in Educational Administration (Commonwealth Council for Educational Administration & Management (CCEAM)), 44*(3).

Taylor, E. S., & Tyler, J. H. (2012). Can teacher evaluation improve teaching? *Education Next, 12*(4), 78-84. Retrieved from https://eric.ed.gov/?id=EJ994601

Techopedia. (2018). *Google docs.* Retrieved from https://www.techopedia.com/definition/13626/google-docs

The Human Rights Campaign Foundation. (2018). *A checklist for a welcoming and inclusive school environment.* Retrieved from http://www.welcomingschools.org/pages/checklist-for-a-welcoming-and-inclusive-school-environment/

The International Society for Technology in Education. (2009). *ISTE standards for administrators.* Retrieved from https://www.iste.org/standards/for-administrators

The International Society for Technology in Education. (2016). *Standards for students.* Retrieved from http://www.iste.org/standards/for-students

References

The International Society for Technology in Education. (2017). *Standards for educators*. Retrieved from http://www.iste.org/standards/for-educators

The International Society for Technology in Education. (2018a). *Be bold with us*. Retrieved from https://www.iste.org/about/about-iste

The International Society for Technology in Education. (2018b). *Essential conditions*. Retrieved From https://www.iste.org/standards/essential-conditions

The International Society for Technology in Education. (2018c). *ISTE standards for education leaders*. Retrieved from https://www.iste.org/standards/for-education-leaders

The Wallace Foundation. (2013). The school principal as leader: Guiding schools to better teaching and learning. *Perspective*, 1-28. Retrieved from http://www.Wallace Foundationfoundation.org/knowledge-center/pages/the-school-principal-as-leader-guiding-schools-to-better-teaching-and-learning.aspx

Tschannen-Moran, M. (2016). *Leadership for successful schools*. San Francisco, CA: Jossey-Bass

Turknett, R.L. & Turknett, C.N. (2005). *Decent People, Decent Company, How to Lead with Character at Work and in Life*. Mountain View, CA: Davies-Black.

University of Kansas-School of Education. (2018). *Timeline of the Individuals with Disabilities Education Act (IDEA)*. Retrieved from https://educationonline.ku.edu/community/idea-timeline

U.S. Department of Education (2007). *25 years of progress in educating children with disabilities through IDEA*. Retrieved from https://www2.ed.gov/policy/speced/leg/idea/history.html

U.S. Department of Education. (2004). *Policy guidance-Access to high school students and information on students by military recruiters*. Retrieved from https://www2.ed.gov/policy/gen/guid/fpco/hottopics/ht-10-09-02a.html

U.S. Department of Education. (n.d.a). *Every Student Succeeds Act (ESSA)*. Retrieved from https://www.ed.gov/esea

U.S. Department of Education. (n.d.b). *Office of civil rights: Resources for LGBTQ students*. Retrieved from https://www2.ed.gov/about/offices/list/ocr/lgbt.html

U.S. Department of Education. (n.d.c). *Family educational rights and privacy act (FERPA)*. Retrieved from https://www2.ed.gov/policy/gen/guid/fpco/ferpa/index.html?src=rn

U.S. Department of Health and Human Services, Health Resources and Services Administration, Maternal and Child Health Bureau. (2014). *The Health and Well-Being of Children: A Portrait of States and the Nation, 2011-2012*. Retrieved from https://mchb.hrsa.gov/nsch/2011-12/health/pdfs/nsch11.pdf

U.S. Department of Education and U.S. Department of Health and Human Services. (2016). *Policy statement on family engagement from the early years to the early grades*. Retrieved from https://www2.ed.gov/about/inits/ed/earlylearning/files/policy-statement-on-family-engagement.pdf

Vaala, S., Ly, A. & Levine, M.H. (2015). *Getting a read on the app store: A market scan and analysis of children's literacy apps.* Retrieved from http://www.joanganzcooneycenter.org/wp-content/uploads/2015/12/jgcc_gettingaread.pdf

Vachon, T. E., & Ma, J. K. (2015). Bargaining for success: Examining the relationship between teacher unions and student achievement. *Sociological Forum, 30*(2), 391-414. doi:10.1111/socf.12168

Valencia, R.R. (2010). *Dismantling contemporary deficit thinking: Educational thought and practice.* DOI: 10.4324/9780203853214

Vaisanen, S., Pietarinen, J., Pyhalto, K., Toom, A., & Soini, T. (2016). Social support as a contributor to student teachers' experienced well-being. *Research Papers in Education, 32*(1), 41-55. doi:10.1080/02671522.2015.1129643

Van Voorhis, F.L., Maier, M.F., Epstein, J.L., & Lloyd, C.M. (2013). *The impact of family involvement on the education of children ages 3 to 8: A focus on literacy and math achievement outcomes and social-emotional skills.* Retrieved from https://www.mdrc.org/sites/default/files/The_Impact_of_Family_Involvement_FR.pdf

Veeriah, J., Piaw, C. Y., Li, S.Y., Hoque, K.E. (2017). Teacher's perception on the relationship between transformational leadership and school culture in primary cluster schools. *Malaysian Online Journal of Educational Management, 5*(4), 18-34. DOI: 10.22452/mojem.vol5no4.2

Vilson, J. (2015). *Empowering educators through cultural competence.* Retrieved from https://www.edutopia.org/blog/empowering-educators-through-cultural-competence-jose-vilson

Vygotsky, L. (1962). *Thought and language.* Cambridge, MA: MIT Press.

Walsh, B. (2014). *Building capacity for family engagement.* Retrieved from https://www.gse.harvard.edu/news/uk/14/11/building-capacity-family-engagement

Walsh, K. (2015). *8 examples of transforming lessons through the SAMR cycle.* Retrieved from, www.emergingedtech.com/2015/04/examples-of-transforming-lessons-through-samr/

Wayman, J. C. (2009). Involving Teachers in Data-Driven Decision-making: Using Computer Data Systems to Support Teacher Inquiry and Reflection. *Journal of Education for Students Placed at Risk (JESPAR), 10*(3), 295-308. doi:10.1207/s15327671espr1003_5

Wayman, J. C., & Jimerson, J. B. (2014). Teacher needs for data-related professional learning. *Studies in Educational Evaluation, 42,* 25-34. doi: 10.1016/j.stueduc.2013.11.001

Wesolowski, B.C. (2015). Tracking student achievement in music performance. *National Association for Music Education.* DOI: 10.1177/0027432115589352

West Corporation. (2018). *About west (schoolmessenger solutions).* Retrieved from https://www.schoolmessenger.com/about/

Wiggins, G. & McTighe, J. (2017). Backwards design. *Learning Theories.* Retrieved from https://www.learning-theories.com/backward-design.html

Williams, R.B., Brien, K., LeBlanc, J. (2012). Transforming schools into learning organizations: Supports and barriers to educational reform. *Canadian Journal of Educational administration and Policy, 134.* Retrieved from https://eric.ed.gov/?id=EJ996773

Wohlstetter, P., Datnow, A., & Park, V. (2008). Creating a system for data-driven decision-making: Applying the principal-agent framework. *School Effectiveness and School Improvement, 19*(3), 239-259. DOI:10.1080/09243450802246376

Wydra, A. (2018). Teachers' unions improve student achievement: Insights from California charter schools. *Chicago Policy Review.* Retrieved from hicagopolicyreview.org/2018/01/20/teachers-unions-improve-student-achievement-insights-from-california-charter-schools/

You, S., Kim, A. Y., & Lim, S. A. (2017). Job satisfaction among secondary teachers in Korea: Effects of teachers' sense of efficacy and school culture. *Educational Management Administration & Leadership, 45*(2), 284-297. doi:10.1177/1741143215587311

Young, N.D., Bonanno-Sotiropoulos, K., & Smolinski, J.A. (2018a). *Making the grade: Promoting positive outcomes for students with learning disabilities.* Lanham, MD: Roman & Littlefield

Young, N.D., Bonanno-Sotiropoulos, K., & Smolinski, J. (2018b). *Achieving Results: Maximizing success in the schoolhouse.* Lanham, MD: Roman & Littlefield

Young, N.D., Jean, E., & Citro, T.A. (2018). *Stars in the schoolhouse: Teaching practices that make a difference.* Wilmington, DE: Vernon Press

Young, N.D., Jean, E., & Mead, A.E. (2019). *From cradle to classroom: A guide to special education for young children.* Lanham, MD: Roman & Littlefield.

Young, N.D., Michael, C.N., & Citro, T.A. (2017). *To campus with confidence.* Madison, WI: Atwood Publishers

Zaretsky, L., Moreau, L., & Faircloth, S. (2008). Voices from the field: School leadership in special education. *The Alberta Journal of Educational Research, 54*(2), 161-177. Retrieved from https://eric.ed.gov/?id=EJ802638

Zascavage, V. (2010). Elementary and Secondary Education Act. In T.C. Hunt, J.C. Carper, T.J. Lasley, II, & C.D. Raisch (eds), *Encyclopedia of Educational Reform and Dissent.* doi: 10.4135/9781412957403.n149

Zepeda, S.J., Parylo, O., & Bengtson, E. (2014). Analyzing principal professional development practices through the lens of adult learning theory. *Professional Development in Education, 40*(2), 295-315. Retrieved from https://eric.ed.gov/?id=EJ1028766

About the Authors

Nicholas D. Young, PhD, EdD

Dr. Nicholas D. Young has worked in diverse educational roles for more than 30 years, serving as a principal, special education director, graduate professor, graduate program director, graduate dean, and longtime superintendent of schools. He was named the Massachusetts Superintendent of the Year; and he completed a distinguished Fulbright program focused on the Japanese educational system through the collegiate level. Dr. Young is the recipient of numerous other honors and recognitions including the General Douglas MacArthur Award for distinguished civilian and military leadership and the Vice Admiral John T. Hayward Award for exemplary scholarship. He holds several graduate degrees including a PhD in educational administration and an EdD in educational psychology.

Dr. Young has served in the U.S. Army and U.S. Army Reserves combined for over 34 years; and he graduated with distinction from the U.S. Air War College, the U.S. Army War College, and the U.S. Navy War College. After completing a series of senior leadership assignments in the U.S. Army Reserves as the commanding officer of the 287th Medical Company (DS), the 405th Area Support Company (DS), the 405th Combat Support Hospital, and the 399th Combat Support Hospital, he transitioned to his current military position as a faculty instructor at the U.S. Army War College in Carlisle, PA. He currently holds the rank of Colonel.

Dr. Young is also a regular presenter at state, national, and international conferences; and he has written many books, book chapters, and/or articles on various topics in education, counseling, and psychology. Some of his most recent books include *Securing the Schoolyard: Protocols that Promote Safety and Positive Student Behaviors* (in-press); *Sounding the Alarm in the Schoolhouse: Safety, Security and Student Well-Being* (in-press); *Embracing and Educating the Autistic Child: Valuing Those Who Color Outside the Lines* (in-press); *The Soul of the Schoolhouse: Cultivating Student Engagement* (in-press); *From Cradle to Classroom: A Guide to Special Education for Young Children* (in-press); *Captivating Classrooms: Student Engagement at the Heart of School Improvement* (in-press); *Soothing the Soul: Pursuing a Life of Abundance Through a Practice of Gratitude* (2018); *Dog Tags to Diploma: Understanding and Addressing the Educational Needs of Veterans, Servicemembers, and their Families* (2018); *Turbulent Times: Confronting Challenges in Emerging Adulthood* (2018); *Guardian of the Next Generation: Igniting the Passion for Quality*

Teaching (2018); *Achieving Results: Maximizing Success in the Schoolhouse* (2018); *From Head to Heart: High Quality Teaching Practices in the Spotlight* (2018); *Stars in the Schoolhouse: Teaching Practices and Approaches that Make a Difference* (2018); *Making the Grade: Promoting Positive Outcomes for Students with Learning Disabilities* (2018); *Paving the Pathway for Educational Success: Effective Classroom Interventions for Students with Learning Disabilities* (2018); *Wrestling with Writing: Effective Strategies for Struggling Students* (2018); *Floundering to Fluent: Reaching and Teaching the Struggling Student* (2018); *Emotions and Education: Promoting Positive Mental Health in Students with Learning* (2018); *From Lecture Hall to Laptop: Opportunities, Challenges, and the Continuing Evolution of Virtual Learning in Higher Education* (2017); *The Power of the Professoriate: Demands, Challenges, and Opportunities in 21st Century Higher Education* (2017); *To Campus with Confidence: Supporting a Successful Transition to College for Students with Learning Disabilities* (2017); *Educational Entrepreneurship: Promoting Public-Private Partnerships for the 21st Century* (2015); *Beyond the Bedtime Story: Promoting Reading Development during the Middle School Years* (2015); *Betwixt and Between: Understanding and Meeting the Social and Emotional Developmental Needs of Students During the Middle School Transition Years* (2014); *Learning Style Perspectives: Impact Upon the Classroom* (3rd ed., 2014); and *Collapsing Educational Boundaries from Preschool to PhD: Building Bridges Across the Educational Spectrum* (2013); *Transforming Special Education Practices: A Primer for School Administrators and Policy Makers* (2012); and *Powerful Partners in Student Success: Schools, Families and Communities* (2012). He also co-authored several children's books to include the popular series *I am Full of Possibilities*. Dr. Young may be contacted directly at nyoung1191@aol.com.

Elizabeth Jean, EdD

Dr. Elizabeth Jean has served as an elementary school educator and administrator in various rural and urban settings in Massachusetts for more than 20 years. As a building administrator, she has fostered partnerships with families, various local businesses, and higher education institutions. Further, she is currently a graduate adjunct professor at the Van Loan School of Education, Endicott College and previously taught at the College of Our Lady of the Elms. In terms of formal education, Dr. Jean received a BS in education from Springfield College; a MEd in education with a concentration in reading from the College of Our Lady of the Elms; and an EdD in curriculum, teaching, learning and leadership from Northeastern University.

Dr. Jean is a primary author on *From Cradle to Classroom: A Guide to Special Education for Young Children* (in-press); *Dog Tags to Diploma: Understanding and Addressing the Educational Needs of Veterans, Servicemembers and their Families* (2018); *Stars in the Schoolhouse: Teaching Practices and Approaches that Make a Difference* (2018); *From Head to Heart: High Quality Teaching Practices in the Spotlight* (2018); *From Lecture Hall to Laptop: Opportunities, Challenges and the Continuing Evolution of Virtual Learning in Higher Education* (2017). She has also written book chapters on such topics as emotional well-being for students with learning disabilities, post-secondary campus supports for emerging adults, parental supports for students with learning disabilities, home-school partnerships, virtual education, public and private partnerships in public education, professorial pursuits, technology partnerships between K-12 and higher education, developing a strategic mindset for LD students, the importance of skill and will in developing reading habits for young children, and middle school reading interventions to name a few. Additionally, she has co-authored and illustrated several children's books to include *Yes, Mama* (2018), *The Adventures of Scotty the Skunk: What's that Smell?* (2014), and *I am Full of Possibilities* Series for Learning Disabilities Worldwide. She may be contacted at elizabethjean1221@gmail.com.

Anne E. Mead, EdD

Dr. Mead has over 35 years of experience in the early childhood education field. Her career has spanned professional roles as a family child care provider, child care center director, preschool special education instructor, early childhood education trainer and consultant on organizational and system management. Dr. Mead is currently the administrator for early childhood programs and extended learning for the Danbury Public Schools in Danbury, Connecticut where she has been credited with the development of a family and community engagement center, before and after school programs, and the formation of a family learning center. She received a BA in Human Services from the University of Connecticut, a MEd in Educational Leadership from National Louis University, and an EdD in Organizational Leadership Studies from Northeastern University.

Dr. Mead has served on numerous local, state and boards related to early childhood education and was a founding member of the National Association for Family, School and Community Engagement She is a member of the Campaign for Grade Level Reading and serves on the family engagement design team for the State of Connecticut State Department of Education. Dr. Mead is a bi-weekly contributor to the Tribuna Newspaper where she writes about family engagement and child education and development. She has written several book chapters about family engagement and is a primary author for the book *From Cradle to Classroom: A Guide to Special Education for Young Children* (in-press). Dr. Mead may be contacted at annemead2003@yahoo.com.

www.ingramcontent.com/pod-product-compliance
Lightning Source LLC
Chambersburg PA
CBHW052049300426
44117CB00012B/2041